HER NAME WAS

Wallis Warfield

Copyright by Man Ray—Courtesy of Harper's Bazaar—International

MRS. WALLIS WARFIELD SIMPSON

HER NAME WAS

Wallis Warfield

BY

EDWINA H WILSON [pseud.]

THE LIFE STORY OF MRS. ERNEST SIMPSON

Illustrated

NEW YORK
E. P. DUTTON & CO., INC.

CONTENTS

❖

LIST OF ILLUSTRATIONS

❖

PUBLISHER'S NOTE

This life story is authenticated by a very close friend of Mrs. Simpson who has known her since childhood, through her school days, her debutante years and her married life in America and in London.

This friend was actually present on many of the occasions recounted in the book. The facts presented here have been checked for accuracy in every detail.

E. P. DUTTON & CO., INC.

HER NAME WAS

Wallis Warfield

Chapter 1

❖

GENERAL INTRODUCTION

THE most famous woman in the world today is neither a leader in public life, nor an heiress, a writer; not a philanthropist, a doctor, a scientist, nor a motion picture star.

Six months ago her name was, comparatively, unknown. Today it echoes above and below the equator— from Baltimore, Md., to the Isle of Bali, from Alaska to the Antipodes.

She is the most romantic figure of the times, the amazing heroine of the most amazing chapter in recent history. Of international figures, she is, at once, the best known and the one known least.

She is, of course, Mrs. Wallis Simpson, the American woman whom half the world expects to become the Queen of England.

There never has been a story like it. There never has been an individual so glamorous. Did Mrs. Simpson take tea on Sunday at Buckingham Palace? Did she drive out on Monday to go shopping? Did she really say thus-and-so to the Duchess? Is it true that she wears a silver fox wrap worth $50,000? Does she, unfailingly, receive 12 dozen American Beauty roses each morning?

Thus the tongues buzz. Thus the world wonders.

Thus, in the United States and the British Empire and the Union of Socialist Soviet Republics, in China and Japan and New Guinea and Madagascar and Cambodia, men and women ask questions, shake their heads, nodding.

They speculate on the future—as shrouded in mystery as, to most of the thousands who speak her name, are the facts of Mrs. Simpson's early life.

Thousands upon thousands of these men and women believe that Wallis Simpson's future, whatever it brings, will affect their own lives.

Suppose—just suppose—an American girl should become Queen of England!

But all that *IS* in the future. The real story of Wallis Simpson begins back in the turning years of the century, in Baltimore, Md. It is the story of a little girl with blue eyes and dark hair, a little girl who could not remember her dead father, whose widowed mother counted her frugal resources sparingly.

In those days her name was Wallis Warfield.

*   *   *   *

She was born June 19, 1896.

The young mother, holding her infant daughter in her arms, looked up at the faces above her, smiled and announced that the baby was to bear her father's name, "Wallis."

"Even though she is a girl," said Mrs. Warfield, "I want her to have his name."

Thus the child was christened—with "Bessie" added as a first name in honor of her mother's sister, Mrs. J. Buchanan Merryman of Washington, D. C., and also for her mother's cousin, Mrs. Alexander Brown of Baltimore.

Teackle Wallis Warfield, who was never to see his daughter, Bessie Wallis (an only child), had died just a few weeks before at Blue Ridge Summit where the young couple had gone, hoping that there his health might be restored. There are men and women in Baltimore today who remember how handsome a pair they were together—T. Wallis Warfield and his bride, the former Alice Montague. Theirs was a love match, youthful and impetuous, though approved by both families. It is still told that Alice Montague, a Virginia beauty, had wealthier suitors. The wealthy young men (there was one in particular) she dismissed, to follow the dictates of her heart and marry T. Wallis Warfield, an exemplary young man of excellent family who had, however, little money. He did not live long enough to acquire much more.

The infant daughter of this couple inherited her mother's wit and gracious manner. In appearance, little Wallis was more like the Warfields—and is to this day. The Mrs. Wallis Simpson whose arrival at a dinner party in London is international news, whose name in the British Court Circular makes headlines around the world, and whose photograph has been published, in recent weeks, more frequently than that of any other living person, would, quite likely, not even be recognized were she to appear on a street in New York or Chicago tomorrow.

She is not tall—about five feet, four inches—though her slenderness seems to give her greater height.

Her face is distinctive for her high cheekbones, which artists invariably admire. Her brow is broad and well-proportioned. Her brown hair (a rich, medium shade) is parted in the center and drawn back in the softest of waves. At the back, the hair is rolled in two coils, crossing each other. There are no hair ornaments in her wardrobe but, on rare occasions, a single diamond gleams in the dark sleekness of her hair.

Her eyes are blue, her skin a creamy, pale tan. She has beautiful teeth of unusual whiteness, and generous lips.

She has, also, small, graceful feet and ankles and has been known to buy 18 pairs of shoes at one time.

Once heard, it is unlikely that anyone would forget her voice. It is low-pitched, distinctive but not at all typically southern.

One who has known her since childhood says of Wallis Simpson, "All her features are good, yet, put together, they do not make beauty. The effect is rather that of a sparkling personality and good nature—more intriguing than beauty."

Another—and there is no one in her intimate circle of friends who knows her better—says: "To me, Wallis' outstanding characteristics have always been her self-discipline, her courage and loyalty. She is very reserved and undemonstrative but, when she does show affection or tenderness, you value it far more than from one who shows emotion easily. She is one of the best judges of people I have ever known. She is extremely subtle, and yet one of her greatest charms is her complete naturalness. I have never seen her make pretenses of any sort."

Wallis Simpson, as all the world knows, lives at 16 Cumberland Terrace, Regent's Park, in London. The house, which she rented for a period of seven months from its owner, Mrs. Cuthbert B. Stewart (absent on a round-the-world tour) happens to stand on land which belongs to the Crown and is leased to building landlords for 100 years or more. Mrs. Stewart is the second lease-holder removed from the Crown authorities.

By a curious coincidence, Wallis Simpson spent much of her childhood in a home that, as Crown property, had been granted to her ancestors by the British monarch. Both of her grandparents, Mr. and Mrs. Henry Mactier Warfield, were born in homes that had been the property of their families since the days of the original grants from the British Crown.

"White Cottage" in Howard County, Md., the birth-place of Mr. Warfield, is part of the original grant to Richard Warfield, first of the family to come to America, in 1662.

"Manor Glen" where Wallis Simpson, as a child, spent many summers, was also an original grant from the British Crown to the ancestors of Anna Emory, who be-came Mrs. Henry Mactier Warfield. Mrs. Warfield was a descendant, through the Emorys, of the well-known Gittings family of Maryland whose ancestral home was known as "Long Green," located in the beautiful Long Green Valley in Baltimore County.

In London, today, guards patrol the street before 16 Cumberland Terrace, Regent's Park. It is reported that, since announcement that Mrs. Simpson was to occupy the house, real estate values in the neighborhood have mounted rapidly. When Mrs. Simpson steps into her motor car to go shopping or to the hairdressers, it is fre-quently necessary to employ ruses to escape the incurably curious.

The letters she receives each morning stack up in piles

higher than the fan mail of many a Hollywood motion picture star.

Her divorce from Ernest Simpson, Oct. 27, 1936, crowded the presidential election and the war in Spain from front page space in newspapers in the United States.

"Wally" she is called in the headlines—but not by her friends.

She does not, as has been reported, call King Edward VIII "David." As does everyone else—except members of the immediate royal family—she addresses him always as "Sir" or "Your Majesty."

A dinner party at Mrs. Simpson's London home is, for those fortunate enough to be invited, an event not to be forgotten. The number of guests on such an occasion is likely to be small—not more than 12 or 14. Mrs. Simpson seldom gives large parties.

Among them, quite likely, might be Lady Diana Duff Cooper, the famous beauty known on the stage some years ago as Lady Diana Manners; her husband, the Rt. Hon. Alfred Duff Cooper, Secretary of State for War; Lord and Lady Louis Mountbatten (Lord Louis is a cousin of King Edward VIII) ; Ramsay MacDonald, the former prime minister of Great Britain; Lady Oxford, better known in America as Margot Asquith, writer and lecturer; Lady Mendl, the American-born Elsie de Wolfe; Alexander Woollcott; Lady Cunard, widow of Sir Bache Cunard; Herr J. von Ribbentrop, the German Ambassador; the Duke and Duchess of Sutherland; John Gunther, European correspondent of the Chicago *Daily News* and author of "Inside Europe."

The guests would be seated about a mirror-topped table, bare of linen of any sort, the center decorated with an arrangement of glass fruits and silver candelabra at either end. Frequently at such dinner parties the table service is pink china—the same pink china dishes on which guests in the home of Wallis Simpson's grandmother, Mrs. Henry Mactier Warfield of Baltimore, were served at the Warfield home on Preston Street. Since the death of her grandmother, the pink china dinner service has been one of Mrs. Simpson's prized possessions.

A butler and two maids would serve the dinner. (Though Mrs. Simpson does not regularly employ a butler, there is always one in attendance for dinner parties.)

A menu of which Mrs. Simpson approves includes:

SMOKED SALMON

CONSOMMÉ

BROOK TROUT AU BUERRE

ROAST GUINEA HEN

COURGETTE   POMME SOUFFLÉ

SALAD

CRÈME BRULÉE

FRUIT

COFFEE

The soup, Mrs. Simpson herself would barely taste, for she does not like it. "Soup," she has said, "is an uninteresting liquid which gets you nowhere." The consommé, however, would be piping hot, served in small cups of black Chinese lacquer, with tiny lids to keep it from cooling. The salad would be on crescent-shaped plates of crystal. Invariably, at such parties, the dessert is elaborate. "I have to have them," Mrs. Simpson explains, "to keep my cook's hand in."

But it is not the food—perfect though it invariably is —or the attractive service that makes a dinner in Mrs. Simpson's home such an occasion. It is the conversation —sprightly, informed, turning to politics, books, art, sports, the theater, or events in the day's news. The hostess, who talks extremely well herself, also listens well. Throughout her life, she has drawn about her, like a magnet, interesting men and women with interesting ideas. No high-brow and making no pretenses at being high-brow, she meets statesmen, authors, actors, peers and peeresses, and old friends from America with equal ease.

With a guest list such as that which has been suggested, the hours after the men have joined the women guests in the living room, would undoubtedly be devoted to further conversation. In entertaining, Mrs. Simpson believes there are two kinds of dinner parties and they should never be mixed; those made up of guests who enjoy games, and those made up of guests who prefer conversation.

Should the guest list include game enthusiasts, the after-dinner hours might be spent at bridge, backgammon or jigsaw puzzles. Mrs. Simpson plays bridge very adequately, but not enthusiastically. She is fond of jigsaw puzzles and expert at them—as is King Edward VIII.

The living room in which Mrs. Simpson entertains is a large one, tastefully but not extravagantly furnished. Always there is an abundance of flowers—tall crystal vases on the mantel, filled with flame-colored lilies or great sprays of brown and pale chartreuse orchids. Always Wallis Simpson has loved flowers and she has a rare ability in arranging them. Her favorites are unusual blossoms in odd shades. Devoted as she is to flowers, she almost never wears them. Occasionally she is seen with a single gardenia pinned to a short mink evening cape.

Her jewels are magnificent—diamonds, emeralds, rubies, aquamarines and sapphires. They are extremely becoming. To see Mrs. Simpson in a gray-blue evening gown of classic simplicity, wearing a necklace and two bracelets made of bands of rubies alternating with clusters of diamonds, is to understand why, instantly upon her entrance, she catches all eyes at balls, in fashionable drawing rooms or at Covent Garden.

Yet this is the same Wallis Simpson—in those days, Wallis Warfield—who, as a 16-year-old school girl, faced the principal of Oldfields, fashionable finishing school at Cockeysville, Md., and confessed, with crimson cheeks and in a trembling voice, that she had hidden two jars of jam beneath her bed and (oh, horrors!) an Edam cheese in her suitcase!

There is a story—and it happens to be a true one—of Wallis Simpson's meeting with King Edward VIII, then H.R.H. the Prince of Wales.

It was in June, 1931—June 10, to be exact. The royal family had assembled in the throne room at Buckingham Palace for an evening of presentations at court. Queen Mary was there in a gown of eastern-blue paillettes and a train to match, lined with blue tissue. She wore a diamond tiara, diamond ornaments and the Order of the Garter across her breast. Princess Mary, the Countess of Harewood, wore white satin and rose point lace with jewelry of sapphires and diamonds. King George and his sons, the Prince of Wales, the Duke of Gloucester, and Prince George, were in full court attire. Attending the court that night, also, was the aged Duke of Connaught, uncle of King George.

The vast room was a glittering array of gold braid and vividly colored uniforms, of women in multi-hued gowns made with court trains, each wearing in her hair the three white plumes and tulle veil that is traditional. Men in military and naval uniforms, diplomats and their ladies from the United States, France, Brazil, Portugal, Chile, Japan, Russia, Venezuela, Bulgaria and a dozen other countries. A scene, the gorgeousness of which is duplicated nowhere else on earth.

Of the men in the room, only King George is seated during the ceremony of the presentations. Standing beside the Prince of Wales was his grand uncle, the Duke of Connaught. Said the Duke, in discreetly muffled tone to the Prince:

"Are there any good numbers tonight?"

Said the Prince, smiling, "I hear that Mrs. Simpson is a very attractive American and I hope to meet her afterward."

Later that night, at a party given by Lady Furness (the former Thelma Morgan and sister of Gloria Vanderbilt) Mr. and Mrs. Ernest Simpson were among the guests. Next morning when the Simpsons' Scotch parlormaid, Kane, went downstairs for the newspapers and mail, the doorman addressed her with marked respect.

"I see," he said, "that you had royalty in your house last night."

"Oh," said Kane, "you mean Mrs. Simpson's three white feathers?"

"Feathers, indeed! Didn't you know Mr. and Mrs. Simpson came home last night in the Prince of Wales' car? Didn't you know it was the Prince himself who brought them?"

Chapter 2

❖

FAMILY . . . CHILDHOOD

THE little girl in the crisp white dress sat very straight in the haircloth covered chair. Her feet, too short to reach the floor, dangled midair. The little girl's dark hair hung about her shoulders, drawn back from her forehead in a pompadour and tied with a blue ribbon. The ribbon matched the color of her eyes, which were very round, just now, and solemn.

"And then, Grandmother—?" the little girl asked.

There was the rustle of stiff black silk as Mrs. Henry Mactier Warfield folded a bit of lace and placed it in the sewing basket beside her. "And then," she answered, "they arrested your Grandfather and took him away, my child. To Fort McHenry first. And then to Fort Munroe."

"But weren't you afraid, Grandmother?"

The woman in the black silk gown looked down at the child. A sudden, changed note came into her voice as she said, "Your Grandfather, Wallis, was a very brave man. He believed he was in the right, and when he was convinced that his cause was just, no amount of opposition could stop him. Yes, those were dreadful times. Dreadful times for everyone. They were war days. But I trusted

22

your Grandfather, and I prayed for him, and the Lord heard my prayers."

The child's eyes, unconsciously, turned to the portrait on the wall. She had heard the story before—many times —but she never tired of it. It made the figure in the portrait so much more real and human. He was a handsome man, if a bit awe-inspiring, with his long, white patriarchal beard and broad forehead. Little Wallis Warfield knew him only in that portrait; he had been dead long before her birth.

Her Grandmother's voice went on, "There were others with your Grandfather, of course. All of them taken prisoner together—all prominent and respected men. There was Mayor George William Brown, Henry May who was in Congress in Washington and Ross Winans and Thomas W. Hall and Teackle Wallis———"

The little girl sat up with a start. "My father!" she exclaimed.

"No, dear. Not your father, but the man for whom he was named. The man for whom you are named, too. Teackle Wallis was a great man and a good man—one of the most scholarly I have ever known. He was a lawyer and provost of the University of Maryland, and in the library you can find the books he wrote. Books about Spain. He was devoted to literature and the language of Spain. Yes, he was with your Grandfather through that year and a half of imprisonment. . . ."

Seated in the Victorian drawing room of her Grandmother's home, on Preston Street in Baltimore, Wallis Warfield listened to the story of her Grandfather's arrest and his refusal to take the oath of allegiance that would have freed him.

It is a story typical of Maryland in Civil War days.

Henry Mactier Warfield, always deeply interested in public affairs, was secretary of the political reform movement in Baltimore in 1859, which was successful in defeating the "Know Nothing Party". As a result, the Democratic Reform Party of Baltimore elected him a member of the "War Legislature" of 1861.

First and foremost, before this legislature, was the question whether Maryland should secede or remain in the Union.

South Carolina, Alabama, Georgia, Louisiana and Texas had entered the Confederacy. Then Virginia, Mississippi, Florida and Tennessee. The situation in Maryland was at white heat. States rights . . . "a sovereign, free and independent nation" . . . the Dred Scott decision . . . Abolitionists . . . Harper's Ferry . . . "personal liberty laws" . . . firing on Fort Sumter . . . "property rights guaranteed by the Constitution"—these are the phrases that thundered on every side.

Henry Mactier Warfield, staunch believer in states rights, with his ancestry stretching back over 200 years as Maryland landholders, was on the side of the South. On the night of Sept. 12, 1861, he and a number of other prominent Baltimoreans who were strongly in favor of the legislature passing a bill to sanction the secession of the state, were arrested by order of General John A. Dix, Federal Department Commander.

They were imprisoned, first at Fort McHenry, later at Fort Munroe, Va., and Fort Warren, in Boston harbor.

For a year and a half Mr. Warfield remained in prison. Then, at last, liberty was offered to him, providing he should first take an oath of allegiance to the government. He declined.

Friends urged his release. A lengthy correspondence began between Mr. Warfield and Secretary of War Stanton, which, today, gives interesting sidelights on the times. In one of these letters, declining to take the oath of allegiance, Mr. Warfield wrote:

"On my part, as I am confined without charge, I renew my claim to be discharged without conditions."

He never did take the oath. At last, at the end of a year and a half of imprisonment, he was released. Although after leaving Fort Warren and returning to Baltimore, he continued to be a strong southern sympathizer, he was, nevertheless, prominent during reconstruction times, not only in business but in a vigorous movement for cleaner politics.

Henry Mactier Warfield established the firm of Henry M. Warfield and Company, exporters of grain and flour. He was one of the original members and one of the first presidents of the Baltimore Chamber of Commerce. He was a director of the Baltimore and Ohio Railroad, and offered the resolution which led to the building of the first Baltimore and Ohio grain elevator, probably the earliest grain elevator constructed in America.

As a boy of 19, he went to Brazil, South America, and later traveled extensively in various parts of the world. He was among the first citizens of the United States to establish a business house in Australia—the firm of Warfield, Rogers and Company which was a branch of his Baltimore organization. His first trip to Australia, it is recorded, was made by sailing vessel and required eight months.

Henry Mactier Warfield, grandfather of Mrs. Wallis Simpson, was a direct descendant of Richard Warfield, first of the family to come to America. Richard Warfield arrived in Maryland in 1662, settling on land granted to him by King Charles II.

The family is known as one of the oldest land owners in the state. Gov. Edwin Warfield, a cousin of Mrs. Simpson's father, was at one time president of the Sons of the American Revolution, and had in his possession one of the earliest deeds to property in Maryland.

The annals of the Warfield family go back to Norman England—and earlier. It was Pagan de Warfield, a Norman gentleman who joined the ranks of William the Conqueror and fought valiantly at the Battle of Hastings, who established the Warfields on English soil. As a reward for his valor and loyalty, Pagan de Warfield received an English manor as "knight's fee." "Warfield's Walk," the estate was called, and in the Domesday Book, Pagan de Warfield is also credited with lands in Stratford.

Robert de Warfield of Warfield House, a knight of the Order of the Garter during the reign of Edward III, was of the Berkshire branch of the family. A second Pagan de Warfield granted Upton to the Prior of Merton as a free gift and this was later known as Warfield Parish.

An order from King John, in 1216, sent to Engelgard de Cygoney who was in charge of Windsor Castle, bade him deliver one Hugh de Polsted to John de Warfield, brother of Elye de Warfield, unless he should meanwhile be ransomed. This John de Warfield lived at Warfield Manor in Warfield's Walk, which was one of 16 "walks" into which Windsor Forest was divided. In the "Annals of Windsor," are found many interesting references to the name of Warfield, indicating the prominence of the family and its association with the royal household.

Centuries later, in Maryland, the names of Upton and Elye appear in the Warfield connection, the family, like many others of English origin, evidently desiring to perpetuate in the new world the names that were familiar and cherished in the mother country.

Richard Warfield, the founder of the American branch of the family, left Berkshire, England, with the Howards and several other Berkshire families, and reached the shores of Chesapeake Bay in 1662. The entire group settled on the banks of the Severn in Anne Arundel County, where they lived in close social and religious association.

A few years after his arrival, Richard Warfield became the proprietor of an estate to which he gave his own name. Later he added to this property tracts patented to him as Warfield's Right, the Increase, the Addition and Warfield's Plains. Within a little more than a quarter of a century, he had acquired, to hand down to his children, a large and rich agricultural area.

Richard Warfield was of the house of Robert de Warfield who bore the crest of the Paschal Lamb. He was a religious man and was a member of the first vestry of old St. Anne's Church, built in accordance with an Act of the Assembly of 1692 which divided the counties into parishes and ordered churches to be built.

The will of Richard Warfield, which was proved in 1703–4, shows that he must have been a man of wealth who surrounded himself with the means of comfortable, and even luxurious, living. In the will are bequests of "silver spoons" and "leather-covered chairs" in large number, services of "new pewter dishes," feather-beds, servants and live stock and many hundreds of acres of land, all proclaiming his material success.

There is also in this will the bequest of "my seal ring to my son John"—surely evidence of the family pride that left to the head of the house the stamp of English lineage.

Richard Warfield's descendants have been prominent in business, politics, the professions of law and medicine and in military affairs. Dr. Charles Alexander Warfield was one of the founders and president of the Medical and Chirurgical Society of Maryland, and one of his sons, Henry, was a member of Congress in 1820.

In the Severn Militia during the Revolutionary War were Captain Benjamin Warfield, Second Lieutenant Robert Warfield, Ensign Charles Warfield, Captain Philemon Warfield, First Lieutenant Launcelot Warfield, Second Lieutenant Thomas Warfield, and Ensign Joseph Warfield.

Dr. Waller Warfield was a surgeon during the Revolutionary War and afterward a member of the Society of the Cincinnati. Elijah and David Warfield were captains in the Fifth Regiment of Maryland Militia.

Probably small Wallis Warfield, sitting in her grandmother's drawing room, long ago in Baltimore, had never even heard the names of these ancestors. Probably, if she had heard them, she would have thought little about them. They had all lived so very long ago.

It was something, though, that Gov. Edwin Warfield of Maryland (in office from 1904 until 1908) should be a relative of hers and that Gov. Andrew Jackson Montague of Virginia (in office from 1902 until 1906) should be a relative of her mother's.

Much more important, in the opinion of six-year-old Wallis Warfield—and a far greater man, too—was her uncle, S. Davies Warfield, who lived with his mother in the house on Preston Street. "Uncle Sol" Warfield who was to become president of the Seaboard Air Line railway, president of the Continental Trust Company of Baltimore and an important figure in the business life of the country, was, at that time, postmaster of Baltimore. He received the appointment from President Cleveland in 1894 and, at the time, was the youngest postmaster in the history of the city.

A close friendship developed between President Cleveland and Postmaster Warfield, and the Baltimorean was frequently called to Washington to give opinions on Maryland affairs. At the end of the Cleveland administration, S. Davies Warfield was reappointed, both by President McKinley and President Theodore Roosevelt.

"Uncle Sol" Warfield was devoted to his niece, Wallis —and remained so throughout his life. He bought her playthings and pets. On pleasant Sunday afternoons they went for walks together. Wallis, an only child, spending much of her time with adults, had a quick wit and lively disposition. Though she admired and respected her grandmother, the house on Preston Street was a much pleasanter place when "Uncle Sol" was about.

S. Davies Warfield never married. He continued to make his home with his mother throughout her lifetime. In his will, in which the bulk of his estate was left to establish a charitable institution to be known as the "Anna Emory Warfield Home for Aged Women" at Manor Glen, his mother's birthplace, he wrote this tribute:

"It was always my desire to be financially able to give my mother every comfort in life, which was the mainspring of my efforts. All of my life up to the time of her death, my mother and myself lived together and I look back to the days of my earliest recollections of anything to the unselfish devotion of my mother to her children, her Christian fortitude and patience through the most trying times, to her wonderful example to us all, and my worship of her as one apart from the world around her.

"To be with my mother was to recognize a supreme influence; therefore—to her memory—I wish to establish this memorial, the Anna Emory Warfield Home for Aged Women."

This home, however, was never built because, after an attempt to break the will on the part of other relatives, it was found that the original fortune of approximately $5,000,000 had shrunk to about $1,000,000.

To Mrs. Wallis Simpson, S. Davies Warfield left at his death, the income from a $15,000 trust fund, accompanied by this notation: "My niece has been educated by me and otherwise provided for by my mother and myself in addition to the provision made herein."

S. Davies Warfield was to leave his name in the history of American railroad development as a member of the organization committee which formed the Seaboard Air Line system. When the system went into receivership in 1908, the successful rehabilitation of the property was credited largely to his efforts as chairman of the receivers. He was also a director and member of the executive committee of the Missouri-Pacific and Western Maryland Railroads. He also organized the group that purchased the Consolidated Gas Company which became the Consolidated Gas, Electric Light and Power Company of Baltimore.

When funeral services for S. Davies Warfield were held, Oct. 25, 1927, in Baltimore, the honorary pall-

A RECENT PORTRAIT OF MRS. SIMPSON
MADE IN VIENNA

bearers included: W. W. Atterbury, president of the
Pennsylvania Railroad; Nicholas Murray Butler, presi-
dent of Columbia University; Arthur Brisbane; Samuel
Untermeyer, and P. A. S. Franklin.

But all that was far in the future as Wallis Warfield,
aged six, ran eagerly to meet her uncle when she heard
his step, as she walked primly beside him in the Sunday
morning parade on Charles Street, and as the three of
them—she and "Uncle Sol" and Wallis' bulldog "Bully"
—romped together on summer afternoons at Manor
Glen.

It was, on the whole, a happy childhood, with a devoted mother; the admonitions of a rather strict, aristo-
cratic grandmother; visits—most exciting!—to and from
Aunt Bessie Merryman in Washington; other small girls
and boys of the neighborhood to play with; and always
"Uncle Sol" to provide exciting surprises.

Thus Wallis Warfield approached her schooldays.

Chapter 3

❖

SCHOOLDAYS

SOMETHING frightful—something utterly dreadful!—
had happened. The girls knew it the moment Miss Nan
arose in the study hall.

The tall figure in dark silk, the hand raised, signaling
for silence, the very erectness of Miss Nan's precise,
snow-white pompadour (each hair exactly in place, as it
invariably was) were signs of warning.

"Girls!" Miss Nan repeated, and there was no possi-
bility of mistaking the tone of voice, "I have something
very serious to say to you. It grieves me to report that I
have found that the strictest rule of this institution is being broken. I have the proof of what I am about to say. I
have seen it with my own eyes. Girls, I find that there
are among you some who have been WRITING LET-
TERS TO BOYS!"

Wallis Warfield, first year student at Oldfield's, fashionable boarding school at Cockeysville, Md., heard this
announcement. Wallis—like 55 other Oldfield's students,
all in the early 'teens, all from prominent Maryland and
Virginia families or others in nearby states—shuddered.

For Oldfield's students knew the rules.

Today, in a charming location with broad lawns, lofty
old trees and, jewel-like, set in the midst of more modern

structures, the eighteenth-century country home that was the original building, is Oldfield's School. Today, as throughout the hundred years and more of its history, it is an institution of the highest standing. Many are the names of women prominent in society, in civic activities, and in philanthropic work who are listed among its alumnae.

But Oldfield's today is a vastly different place from what it was in 1912 when Wallis Warfield arrived for her first taste of life in boarding school.

Presiding over the institution was Miss Nan McCulloch, in whose family Oldfield's has continued since its beginnings. Miss Nan, in spreading black silk skirts, in gowns that rose to collars, high-boned to her earlobes, who wore always a small black cashmere shawl about her shoulders, did not compromise in her views about the training of young women.

Those entrusted to her care learned, first of all, to conduct themselves at all times in a quiet and decorous manner. They learned the etiquette and manners which Miss Nan herself had been taught as a girl. First year students, each morning when they faced the principal for the day, curtsied deeply. "Old girls"—those who had been there a year or more—might kiss her cheek. Oldfield's students learned, too, to be devout in religious observance. Their course of study and classroom recitations were those considered necessary to train young women for a dignified introduction to society.

On the door of each room in the school dormitory was a placard reminder:

"Gentleness and courtesy are expected of the girls at all times."

It was due to this placard that the school's two basketball teams (they were not allowed to play games in competition with other schools) were known as "Gentleness" and "Courtesy."

Wallis Warfield played on the "Gentleness" team, and played a right good game, too. She was not, however, particularly enthusiastic about basketball. She played it as she has played at other sports throughout her life—always well, but never with the overwhelming enthusiasm that makes such activities the major interest in life for so many young people—and older ones.

*   *   *   *

There is little likelihood that, of those who heard Miss Nan McCulloch make that horrifying pronouncement, "Girls, I find that there are among you some who have been writing to boys," in the study hall at Oldfield's that morning in 1912, not one has forgotten.

Writing letters to boys WAS one of the most sternly forbidden of forbidden pleasures in the school.

Awe over the enormity of the charge . . . guilty knowledge that caused hearts to beat in double-time and cheeks to flush . . . dismay over the impending consequences. With such thoughts fifty-six girls listened as Miss Nan continued:

"Tomorrow I want every girl in the school who has broken this rule to come to my room and confess."

In small groups they gathered later and discussed it. In the privacy of their own rooms girls, in twos and threes, sat in sober-faced conclave. What would happen now? Would the guilty ones be expelled? Would there be the black shame of packing, of having the doors of the school close behind them, of returning home and, disgraced, facing parents who must hear the truth?

Low-voiced, the whispering buzzed on.

Next morning, the ominous day of confession. One by one, the timid approach to Miss Nan's quarters. The slow-spoken, hesitant, "I—I'm so terribly sorry. I'll never do it again—Miss Nan—honestly, I won't! But I —I did!"

Fifty-six girls in the school. Fifty-four confessions.

It was that morning that Wallis Warfield, making a clean breast of her guilt, heard Miss Nan McCulloch continue (perhaps with a bit of dry humor) :

"While you are about it, Wallis, is there anything further you have to confess?"

A pause. Then, in a slow voice, "Yes, Miss Nan. I have two jars of jam—I brought them from home the last time I was there—in my room. They're under the bed. And an Edam cheese in my suitcase."

The day, with its mass confessions, passed. There were no frightful consequences. No one was expelled. But the importance of Oldfield's rules—and the importance of abiding by them—had been emphasized, unforgettably.

There was another day when Miss Nan arose in the study hall and made an announcement—quite a different one.

"Girls," she began, in a clear voice, her face cameolike, her light gray eyes unable to conceal the amusement her voice hid, "it seems that a curious epidemic has broken out in the school. I understand that a number of you, fully appreciating the desirability of a slender figure, have set about to lose weight and that, to do this, you have been taking doses of cod liver oil. Will all those who have cod liver oil in their possession please turn it over to the infirmary?"

Going to Oldfield's meant, to Wallis Warfield, separa-
tion from her mother for the first time in her life—for
a period of any length. Before that, Wallis had attended
Arundel School in Baltimore, a private day school for
small boys and girls in the primary classes and for girls
alone in the more advanced grades.

Arundel School does not exist today. It stood on Chase
Street, just west of Charles, easily within walking distance from Wallis' home at 212 Biddle Street—not far,
either, from her grandmother's address on Preston.

In 1908 Mrs. Warfield had married John Freeman
Raisin Jr., son of the Democratic Party leader of Baltimore. Newspaper reports of the marriage ceremony
mention that "the beautiful young daughter of the
bride" attended her mother.

John Freeman Raisin Jr. died two years later. Widowed for a second time, Mrs. Raisin's interest—even
more than most mothers'—centered in her daughter.
The two were unusually devoted—and remained so always.

Mrs. Raisin saw to it that Wallis, as a youngster, always wore crisp, fresh schooldresses, that her hair-ribbons
stood up in perky bows, that she was off promptly each
morning in time to reach Arundel School by nine o'clock.

Arithmetic, spelling, geography, history. Sums on the
blackboard. Transitive verbs and intransitive. Particip-
ial phrases and compound sentences. "The state of
Maryland is bound on the north by Pennsylvania, on the
east by Delaware and the Atlantic Ocean, on the south
by Virginia . . ."

Wallis Warfield, as every Maryland school child,
learned how great names and deeds of the past have been
associated with the state. Lord Baltimore, who founded

the colony in 1632, endowing it with traditions of tolerance and independence; Charles Carrol of Carrolton, the fiery, intrepid signer of the Declaration of Independence; Fort McHenry and Francis Scott Key who saw "the rockets' red glare, the bombs bursting in air" and wrote the national anthem, "The Star Spangled Banner"; Edgar Allan Poe and the house where he lived and his grave.

There is another story—peculiarly Baltimore's own—that Wallis Warfield must have learned.

It is the story of a charming girl, beautiful and spirited, born in the city of sedate red brick houses and snow-white doorsteps 150 years ago. Betsy Patterson—the belle of a society the like of which has not flourished since. Betsy Patterson who, at 18, had suitors from north and south, east and west, who was known for her sparkling wit and her cleverness as well as her physical loveliness.

Beautiful Betsy Patterson who fell in love with a Prince——

He was Captain Jerome Bonaparte, brother of Napoleon Bonaparte, the first Consul of France. Handsome and dashing and debonair, he came to America in 1803 and, in September, arrived in Baltimore in time for the races. (Then, as today, a Maryland tradition.)

It was Samuel Chase, another signer of the Declaration of Independence, who introduced them and, for both, from that moment of first meeting the rest was inevitable. Soon Betsy Patterson and Captain Bonaparte were engaged. Betsy's father, the doughty William Patterson, stormed. He sent his daughter away to forget— but she only remembered the more, and swore she "would rather be Jerome's wife for an hour than the wife of another for eternity."

William Patterson continued to forbid the marriage— but Betsy had a way with her. At last, though still grudgingly, he succumbed to her persuasion. The ceremony took place on Christmas Eve, and never was there a happier young couple.

Their gaiety, as historians have recorded, was "dancing over a volcano." Napoleon heard the news and was in a rage. Finally the verdict came. Captain Jerome Bonaparte was to return to France at once with these added instructions:

"What the First Consul has prescribed, in the most positive manner, is that all captains of French vessels be prohibited from receiving on board the young person to whom the Citizen Jerome has connected himself, it being his intention that she shall, by no means, come to France, and it is his order that, should she arrive, she shall not be suffered to land, but be sent back to the United States."

Heart-sick, Jerome and Betsy decided to obey the edict. They sailed from Philadelphia, with an aunt as chaperone. But ill luck was soon upon them. First, the ship was wrecked off the Delaware coast and they were obliged to delay their voyage.

In 1804 Napoleon Bonaparte was made Emperor and letters to his brother grew more violent in their denouncements. Why had Captain Bonaparte not obeyed his Emperor's orders?

At last the young couple reached Lisbon where a French guard prevented her landing. Jerome, vowing undying love, set off for Paris to win permission from his brother for Betsy to enter France.

Betsy Patterson Bonaparte never saw her husband again.

Forbidden to step on French soil, she went to England and, at Camberwell, near London, her son was born. She christened him Jerome Napoleon Bonaparte. Bitter and humiliating months passed, with scant word from Jerome. Alone, in a strange country, the young mother showed a stanch and courageous nature to be marveled at.

But the blow was to fall—

Napoleon tried to force the Pope to annul the marriage of Betsy and Jerome; the Pope refused. Napoleon, thereupon, ordered French courts to declare the marriage null and void. They did—and weak, fickle Jerome went through a second marriage, dictated by his brother.

Betsy returned to Baltimore to live there until old age—a figure of mystery, tragedy and romance.

That is the story that Wallis Warfield, as every other Baltimore school child, must have learned. It is a story to be recalled for its similarity—in part, at least—with events of the times. But today there are differences, as well as similarities. Jerome Bonaparte has written his name in history as a weakling, as one to accept, with servility, the dictation of others, as a prince who was without royalty and who broke faith with his love.

*　　　*　　　*　　　*

Wallis Warfield spent two summers at Miss Charlotte Noland's Camp for Girls, at her home, Burland, near Middleburg, Va.—the estate which today is owned by William Ziegler.

It was several years later that Miss Noland established Foxcroft, which today is so outstanding among fashionable and exclusive schools for girls in America.

The camp which Wallis Warfield and about 20 other girls, almost all from Baltimore, attended, was in no sense a school. It was designed for recreation, wholesome and out-of-doors—a place so delightful that, invariably, young charges, obliged to return home, wept.

At Miss Noland's there was horseback riding and swimming and games, picnics and parties. There were small, rustic cottages and—for "old girls" who had been there before—the "tepee," a tent, to live in which was the absolute summit of ambition of every girl at Burland.

There was, too, "The Flying Yankee"—an old eighteenth century coach of amazing size and elegance into which 21 girls could—and did—crowd, all in their best, be-ruffled summer frocks and flower-decked straw hats, as, with Miss Noland, they set off to attend garden parties in the neighborhood.

Oh, yes, summers at Burland were, indeed, to be remembered!

The name "The Flying Yankee" was painted on the sides of the coach. There was another vehicle, unnamed and much less impressive, to ride in which was even more of a treat to Wallis Warfield and her particular circle of friends.

This was a carriage, owned by the parents of a young man named Lloyd Tabb. He was Wallis' first beau—a lad about 17 years old, whose parents' home was named "Glenora." Here Wallis and her friends often were invited to play tennis and attend Sunday evening suppers. "Glenora" impressed the girls particularly because, among other decorations in the living room, there was an altogether life-like stuffed owl.

Lloyd's guests invariably paused to pay their respects to his grandmother, arrayed in a ruffled white tea gown

trimmed with lavender ribbons, as she enjoyed the afternoon from her comfortable chair on the lawn.

The equipage which transported the girls to and from
"Glenora" was drawn by a horse with the somewhat
strange name of "Almo Dobbin Spec Creature." There
was a song about this animal which the young campers
used to sing. It was an original composition and it went
like this:

"Almo, sweet Almo, where have you been?
 What is your home, dear? What is your phone, dear?
 Your number please give.
 A wedding ring is the only ring that Almo can hear."

Fragments of another melody, sung in those by-gone
days, are recalled today. It is a song which was part
of an amateur variety show which the girls at Burland
presented. All—or almost all—of Middleburg attended the performance which was given in the town
hall. It was a rather hastily rehearsed program, repre-
senting the respective talents of 20 girls ranging in age
from 12 to 16 years.

The number in which Wallis Warfield took part was
a sort of tableau. One girl, dressed as a dapper young
man, appeared on the stage and sang a song called,
"Dear, Delightful Women." When the chorus was
reached the "dear, delightful women" appeared, one
by one, as they were named in the song:

"Dear, delightful women, how I simply love them all.
 If they're bad, if they're bold,
 If they're coy, if they're cold——"

So the words went—the "bad," the "bold," the "coy" and the "cold" stepping out from the wings in turn. One of these ravishing creatures (there appears to be no record which one) was Wallis Warfield, attired, like the others, in borrowed evening gowns, too large, no doubt, but very fine to 14-year-old eyes.

Middleburg liked the show, too, and applauded. Afterward there was dancing and the evening ended (rather early) as a distinct success.

Other events at Burland, still remembered, are the times the girls, invited to a garden party in Middleburg, were obliged to walk a mile to their destination; the times they went coon hunting and gigging for frogs; the time, on their way to go swimming, they crossed a cornfield and killed a black snake; "hobble skirt races" (hobble skirts were in vogue then) when they tied hair-ribbons about their pleated skirts and raced for a goal.

Burland—yes, Burland, indeed, where, from morning until night, the hours were crowded and care-free— where days were all sunlight and blue skies, and life itself as dream-like and guileless as the trail of a velvet-winged butterfly through tall, nodding poppies.

But summers at Burland, alas—as elsewhere—came to an end. In September there was Oldfield's again, where the rising bell rang, unfailingly, at seven a. m., and, from then on until "lights out," hours of the day were apportioned in a schedule far different from the easy routine at camp.

There were no beaux, no "date nights" at Oldfield's. Visits from brothers, even, had to be arranged with some care.

Students were allowed two week-ends in town yearly, providing they made a certain average in scholarship.

If any student received a letter from a young man, she was instructed to take it to Miss Nan.

Students were required to make their own beds (a task which Wallis Warfield loathed).

For going out on a wet day without rubbers the penalty was to learn a specified number of lines of poetry.

These were a few of the rules.

Religious education was given its full share of attention. Each day upon arising, five minutes were set apart for silent prayer. At the breakfast table, Miss Nan said grace. On Sundays, immediately after breakfast, the girls memorized the Collect and Gospel for the day. Then, walking two by two, attended by members of the faculty, they attended church.

Sunday dinner was served on their return from church. Afterward, one at a time, the girls appeared before Miss Nan to recite the Collect and Gospel, learned in the morning. Evensong, at 5:30 in the little stone chapel on the hill, was not obligatory, but everyone attended hymns after supper. "Hymns" was generally considered the most enjoyable part of the day, when each girl might suggest favorite religious songs and the whole group sang them.

During Lent, in particular, religious observances were marked. At 6:30 in the morning many a girl arose and, mid ice and snow, climbed the hill to the stone chapel to make devotions before breakfast. Each student, of course, made some Lenten sacrifice—usually of food, which to a school girl, is a sacrifice indeed.

But there was fun, too. Coasting in the winter . . . visiting in the pleasant intimacy of the dormitory after study hours . . . boxes from home . . . school plays . . . school parties . . . basketball . . .

There was a Sunday when nine girls from Oldfield's—including Wallis Warfield—accompanied by a teacher, set off for a walk. They passed a deserted old house with some of its windows broken. The temptation of those windows was too much! Someone picked up a stone and let it fly. A moment later, nine young ladies—far from sedate—were hurling missiles through the air. Their aim was excellent. Before the excitement ended, amid resounding sounds of smashing glass, 17 more windows showed gaping holes.

The nine had "had their fling," literally, and, without delay were to learn that, for such, there is a price.

For two weeks they were not allowed to join the other girls after study hours—easily the best part of the day. The guilty nine, instead, sat in a classroom, listening while an instructor read aloud to them. The first evening when, at the end of the hour's reading, the girls arose to go, they said goodnight politely and spoke about how interesting the book had been.

"Really?" exclaimed the instructor, "I'm surprised, because I picked the dullest one I could find!"

Nevertheless, the reading continued for two weeks. The punishment—well calculated—for the spirited young culprits was to be boredom.

*　　*　　*　　*

Nothing could be a lovelier sight than May Day at Oldfield's. It was the climax of the year, in those days assuming the importance which today attaches to Commencement.

The countryside, on May Day, was newly green. The dogwood was in bloom and the carpet-like lawn, sloping down to the little wooded dell at the foot of the hill, provided a natural amphitheater for the truly beautiful ceremony.

The entire student body took part. The May Queen, elected by popular vote and amid much excitement, had chosen her court of attendants. Parents and relatives and friends and alumnae had arrived. The school was in a froth of last-minute bustle and anxiety and activity.

Then—suddenly—from open windows, from the top of the hill, came girlish voices, lifted high in the May Song; slowly, winding its way down the hillside, came the procession. First, the May Queen, in gleaming white, looking proud and young and lovely. Then her attendants, two by two. Lastly, the rest of the students, each wearing white, each carrying flowers to be presented to the Queen.

> "Flowers of tender hue
> We pick, dear Queen
> This day for you—"

Young voices chanted the song, placing the flowers before the Queen. Young faces, young hearts, a young world. It was all stirring and beautiful and a little exciting. Seventeen-year-old Wallis Warfield, taking part in this pageantry, must have felt its spell. She must have felt, too, vague regrets over saying goodbye—for youth's regrets, usually, are vague.

Wallis was not returning to Oldfields next fall. It was a goodbye—to childhood.

Chapter 4

❖

DEBUTANTE DAYS

THE headlines were alarming—inch-high, in black type; "RUSSIANS ATTACK BRESLAU FORTS WHILE FRENCHMEN AIM AT FREEBURG"; "ALLIES BEGIN A FORWARD MOVEMENT—BIG GUNS FIRING ALONG WHOLE FRONT"; "GERMANS ON NEW BATTLE LINE IN POLAND—REINFORCEMENTS FROM WEST—A NEW GERMAN ARMY MOVES ON PIOLRKOW——"

Of course, everyone said, there wasn't a chance for the United States to become involved in the war, frightful as it was. The United States had troubles enough at home, without borrowing more in Europe. There was wide-spread sympathy for devastated Belgium and Red Cross drives were in progress. Food and clothing and hospital supplies were being packed and loaded on ships. Women made bandages and signed petitions and contributed to relief funds.

There was talk of "Preparedness" by those who thought that national defenses were inadequate and those who thought they were not . . . President Wilson discussed with Ambassador Herrick plans to aid destitute non-combatants . . . Ex-president Theodore Roosevelt wrote to the New York *Times* about conditions in Mexico

46

1, 2, 4, © E. P. D. Co.; 3, *Acme*

SCHOOLDAY SNAPSHOTS AND HER CHILDHOOD HOME

In 1, Wallis Warfield can be seen at the extreme right, in 2 second from left, and in 4, left group, right.

where General Villa's followers had sent President Carranza fleeing . . . Assistant Secretary of Navy Franklin D. Roosevelt made an address before the National Civic Federation . . . From Washington, D. C., came news that: "The navy has completed its new wireless chain. Eventually Washington will be able to reach its warships anywhere in the world."

Three thousand miles away from all this, across the black Atlantic, a boyish-looking young English officer was seeing action at the front for the first time. H.R.H., the Prince of Wales, first lieutenant in the Grenadier Guards, was reported by news services to be "looking fit in spite of the enormous amount of work he manages to cram into the hours from daybreak until sometimes almost daybreak. One of his favorite habits is to vanish, to be discovered several hours later, interrogating wounded men in out-of-the-way corners." The Prince wrote letters to his mother, Queen Mary, that were opened and passed by official censors, as those of any other British soldier. The Prince went about his duties as any young lieutenant. He was seeing war for the first time, as all Europe, in December, 1914, was seeing war.

And, in the United States——

The Colorado mine strike was being investigated . . . Mr. and Mrs. Vernon Castle's dancing was thrilling Broadway audiences, and a new play, "The Miracle Man" by George M. Cohan, had opened . . . Women suffragists paraded in New York and Chicago . . . Eddie Pullen won an automobile race at Corona, Cal., over a 300.3 mile course, setting a new world mark for road racing—87.4 miles an hour . . . High-laced shoes with cloth tops were a new feminine fashion . . . Newspapers printed lessons in auction bridge. . . .

There was a new book out that fall, a novel called
"His Royal Happiness," written by Mrs. Everard Cotes.
The book was advertised as "a timely and startling international romance, relating the dramatic complications
which arise when a Prince of England happens to fall
in love with the daughter of the President of the United
States." Reviewers called the volume, "a charming love
story" with "a daring theme."

Did Wallis Warfield, spending her first year out of
school days, read that book? Probably not. There were
so many, many other things for a girl about to come out
in society to think about, so many other things to do
besides reading books. Shopping and luncheons and
matinees. Talking over the party the night before, talking over the one to come. Telephone calls and flowers
arriving, and invitations.

Miss Warfield was one of 49 debutantes to be formally
presented that year at the first Monday german of the
Bachelors' Cotillion Club, on December 7.

For a girl reared in Baltimore, social debuts are made
invariably at the Bachelors' Cotillion. It is a tradition to
be compared only with that of the Saint Cecilia Society
in Charleston, N. C. In Charleston, as in Baltimore, each
season's "buds" make their bows together, at one gala
ball. It is, for eighteen-year-olds, the night of nights—
to be tremblingly anticipated, treasured in memory.

But in December, 1914, battlefields, even 3,000 miles
away, had cast their gloom over Baltimore, as over other
American cities. Earlier in the fall a Baltimore society
editor had written:

"Entertainments to be given this season for and by
debutantes are likely to be marked by a simplicity not
known in Baltimore for a generation or more. Thirty-

four of the 'buds' who will make their bows this year have signed an agreement, insuring an absence of rivalry in elegance in respective social functions, and pledging the signers and their families to refrain from extravagance in entertaining."

Wallis Warfield was among the 34 who signed this pledge. Later her uncle, S. Davies Warfield, president of the Seaboard Air Line Railway, busy with relief work and charitable organizations, stated that, "the report that he will give a large ball for his debutante niece, Miss Wallis Warfield, is without foundation in that he does not consider the present a proper time for such festivities, when thousands are being slaughtered in Europe."

But "Uncle Sol" Warfield was ever ready to escort his niece and her friends where they wished to go. To the 18-year-olds, it was quite an occasion to ride in state in S. Davies Warfield's big limousine, driven by a chauffeur, to be seen with the distinguished-looking older man.

Wallis and her friends frequently drove in another impressive automobile. It belonged to young Carter G. Osburn—or rather, to his father. Today Osburn is an automobile salesman at Cockeysville, Md. He was one of the young men with whom Wallis played tennis and golf and danced at the Country Club the summer of 1914. He was—and today admits it—badly smitten.

Some of the events listed in Wallis Warfield's engagement book that fall were:

Nov. 5—Football dance at the Catonsville Country Club.

Nov. 6—Luncheon at the Stafford Hotel, given by Mrs. William R. Eareckson for her debutante daughter, Miss Augusta Eareckson.

Nov. 13—Oyster roast given by Albert Graham Ober

for his debutante niece, Rebecca Ober, at his country place in the Green Spring Valley at 1 p.m. The evening of the same day, the party given by Mr. and Mrs. Frederick B. Beacham for their daughter, Priscilla Beacham, at Lehmann Hall, at which Wallis Warfield assisted in receiving the guests.

Nov. 17—Luncheon at the Baltimore Country Club for Miss Carolyn H. McCoy, given by her mother, Mrs. Kent McCoy.

Nov. 19—Luncheon at the Baltimore Country Club given by Mrs. Henry C. Kirk, Jr., for her daughter, Miss Mary Kirk.

Nov. 25—Luncheon given by Mrs. Edwin H. Truist at her home on N. Calvert St., for her debutante granddaughter, Miss Rena Alverda Sawyer.

Nov. 28—Trip to Philadelphia with Miss Priscilla Beacham to spend the week-end with friends and attend a football game.

Dec. 2—Luncheon given for Miss Eleanor Cole Bosley by her mother, Mrs. John C. Bosley, at the Baltimore Country Club.

Dec. 3—Luncheon given by Mrs. Hugh Lennox Bond at her home for her debutante daughter, Jessie Van Rensselaer Bond.

Dec. 7—The Bachelors' Cotillion.

*   *   *   *

Baltimore's Lyric Theater that night had been transformed, according to a newspaper report, into "a bower of beauty where light and color mingled to form an almost tropical atmosphere of warmth and fullness of life." The floor of the theater had been cleared of seats. Surrounding the large hall were the boxes, with nets

draped beneath them in which the debutantes' flowers—
bouquet on bouquet—created the effect of a continuous
garland. The stage had been transformed into a garden-
like supper room, reached from the dance floor by satin
pillows, serving as steps.

There is a story, told by Baltimoreans, about these
pillows. It is said that, in days before the Civil War, the
proud Marylanders, refusing to surrender to the poverty
that was a common lot, contrived to maintain their social
traditions. Spending money on anything so extravagant
as decorations for the Bachelors' Cotillion, however, was
out of the question. So Baltimore matrons ripped up their
ball gowns—worn to shabbiness—and made them into
cushions to give elegance to the scene of their daughters'
presentation to society. Ever since those days there have
been silken cushions for the slippered feet of dancers at
the Cotillions.

But back to the night of Dec. 7, 1914——

Wallis Warfield arrived at the Cotillion with her
mother's cousin, Mrs. George Barnett of Washington, as
chaperon and with two partners—Major General
George Barnett, U. S. Marine Corps, and her cousin,
Henry M. Warfield Jr. Wallis wore a gown of white
satin combined with chiffon and trimmings of pearls.
The chiffon veiled the shoulders and fell in a knee-length
tunic, banded in pearl embroidery—a style similar to
the gowns in which Mrs. Vernon Castle danced so grace-
fully. Her flowers were American Beauty roses. Mrs.
Barnett, her chaperon, wore a gown of cloth of gold with
touches of turquoise and diamonds.

Forty-nine debutantes waiting for the exciting moment to arrive. Forty-nine young girls, each wearing a
new dress and carrying flowers, trying to look serene and

calm, aware that the event was the most important, to date, of their brief lives.

The band struck up the first number. Partners turned to partners. The Cotillion was on!

News columns next morning reported that, "The first Monday german of the Bachelors' Cotillion Club was held at the Lyric last night and, despite the shadows which gathered over society when the war began, the great opening event of the season was one of charm and happiness and, of course, of beauty."

To older men and women, doubtless, it was just another Cotillion. To 49 debutantes, bright-eyed, hearts singing, smiling at partners as they danced, it was the threshold of a new world—a world that surely would match the Cotillion itself in glamor and color and excitement.

*   *   *   *

Three days later Wallis Warfield assisted in receiving at "one of the largest receptions of the season." She saw the Princeton Triangle Club's performance at Albaugh's Lyceum the night of Dec. 24. The play was "Fie! Fie! Fi-Fi," a decided hit. Critics wrote of it, "Much of the entertainment was due to the clever lyrics of F. Scott Fitzgerald who has written some excellent 'patter songs'."

Christmas night, Dec. 25, the second german was held at the Lyric. The debutantes and their partners, their parents and their parents' friends danced that night to this musical program:

One-step, "I Want to Go Back to Michigan"; Waltz, "Flora"; One-step, "Tsin-Tsin"; One-step, "Land of My Best Girl"; The german, waltz, "Heart O'Mine"; Fox-trot, "Reuben"; Waltz, "The Skaters"; One-step, "When

It's Night Time in Burgundy"; Waltz, "Please"; Foxtrot, "Old Folks' Rag"; One-step, "When You Wore a Tulip"; Waltz, "Millicent."

There were other Cotillions—January 18, February 1 and February 15. There were other parties and dinners and luncheons and receptions. Invariably, where the younger set gathered, Wallis Warfield was noticed for her style and distinction. One of her evening gowns, remembered today, was made with a bodice of cloth of gold, figured with little flowers and a full skirt of crepe de chine in a shade called "sunset color." Wallis was wearing her hair in a new way that season, waved softly at the sides, with a French roll from the forehead to the crown of the head and coiled in a knot at the back.

She had plenty of admirers. Tony Biddle of Philadelphia was one. He came to Baltimore with Reggie Hutchinson and a number of other Philadelphia youths to attend a birthday party. The boys had to return to classes at Yale in a few days and when they left there were sad good-bys.

Later—in the spring—there was a Campus Club houseparty at Princeton where a number of Baltimore young men were students; De Coursey Orrick, Bryan and Bill Dancy; Tom Hilliard; Charles Kock; Bill McAdoo whose father was Secretary of the Treasury in President Wilson's cabinet. Duly chaperoned, the girls went to dance at the Colonial Club and to the Ivy for tea.

The spring and the summer slipped by. August and then September, and a new social season——

But not for Wallis Warfield. Her grandmother, Mrs. Henry Mactier Warfield, had died and Wallis, in mourning, did not accept invitations. She and her mother were living in an apartment at Earl Court. Mrs. D. Buchanan Merryman came to spend part of the winter with them.

Wallis did not attend the Bachelors' Cotillions in 1915. In the winter, though, she went to visit her cousin, Mrs. Henry Mustin, at Pensacola, Fla. Lieut. Henry Mustin was an instructor in the naval aviation school there. Pensacola was a place of excitement and activity; of gorgeous sunshine and the blue, blue ocean; of young men in uniforms who risked their lives recklessly, sky-rocketing through the air; of war talk and whispered rumors; and official teas and dances.

And there Wallis Warfield met Lieut. E. Winfield Spencer, Jr.

Chapter 5

❖

ROMANCE AND MARRIAGE

THE room was a hum of voices—low-pitched, even, with now and then a feminine exclamation—rushing, staccato —and a rumble of laughter. Tall young men in uniforms and others in civilian clothes, talking to women whose bright-hued gowns made splashes of brilliant color. Older men, handsome, with snow-white hair and the gold braid of authority. Older women in little groups, nodding, smiling.

The musicians lingered over their instruments, but soon they would be playing again. It was an orchestra that played fox-trots with a verve, though so many of the older dancers thought the fox-trot undignified and the new tunes even worse. But then, many things were changing these days. . . .

*   *   *   *

She stood near a window—a slender, graceful girl wearing a pale blue gown. She was talking to two young men in uniform and her eyes, bluer than the dress she wore, shone, star-like, as she turned, smiling up at the taller young man beside her. She held a pink rose, nodding on a slender stem, in her hand.

The young man in the doorway halted. He was a

young man in the uniform of a naval lieutenant, on his shoulders the insignia of the air corps. There was dash to the set of those shoulders, jauntiness of an indefinable sort in the way he stood. He was a tall young man, compactly built and handsome. He had dark eyes and hair and a small mustache.

"Who," asked the lieutenant, touching the arm of his companion, "is the girl in the blue dress?"

The other turned. "You mean over there by the window? Oh, that's Miss Warfield. From Baltimore, I believe. She's a friend of Lieutenant Mustin's wife—or maybe a relative. They say she's as clever as she is good-looking. Look, over there's that chap from Boston I was telling you about who wants to meet you. Shall we go over and—why—well, I'll be——!"

There was no use saying more, for the lieutenant was no longer beside him. The lieutenant was half-way across the room, making his way toward the girl in blue.

*   *   *   *

Lieut. Earl Winfield Spencer Jr. looked down at the girl with whom he was dancing.

"So you've never been in Florida before, Miss Warfield," he said. "How do you think you're going to like it?"

"I do like it—very much. I think it's lovely here."

"Yes, Florida sunshine's the real thing, isn't it? Great, when you're accustomed to the sort of winters we have in Chicago."

"Is Chicago your home?"

"Well, it has been. Highland Park is where my family live—that is, my father and mother. But I've drifted around a good deal. Never know, in the navy, where you'll be tomorrow. I'm glad, though, that you like Florida. Are you going to be here for a while?"

"Oh, a few weeks."

"That's good news. Pensacola's quite a place—interesting, really. I hope you'll let me show you about. Have you seen the aviation school yet?"

"Yes. It's fascinating! Lieutenant Mustin took us the day after I arrived."

"Lieutenant Mustin is a good friend of mine, fine fellow."

"Yes, isn't he! His wife is my cousin. I'm visiting them."

"Then would you think it impertinent of me to ask if the four of us could have dinner together—say, tomorrow night?"

The girl looked up, smiling. "I wouldn't think it impertinent of you, at all, Lieutenant Spencer," she said. "But I have an engagement for tomorrow evening. I'm sorry."

"Then how about the next night?"

"I'm not sure whether Corinne has something planned or not. You might telephone——"

"I will. I'll telephone the first thing in the morning."

"Oh, but not too early, please!"

"What time, then? At nine o'clock, ten o'clock, eleven? I want to know when I'm going to see you again. I'm afraid I'm going to be impatient about that. There are a lot of things I'd like to talk to you about. A lot of things——"

Abruptly—on a shrill note—the music ended. Lieutenant Spencer's words were lost as another girl greeted his partner. In a moment she was the center of a group. Someone spoke and Wallis Warfield made a quick retort.

There was laughter and the group widened as another officer joined them.

"My dance next, Wallis," he announced. "I hope you haven't forgotten. I've asked Harry to play that Victor Herbert waltz you like so much——"

*   *   *   *

Blue sky and white clouds floating lazily over-head. Yellow sunshine that dripped over the Florida landscape as though it had been painted. A level expanse of shore and, beyond, the blue, blue water. Back near the hangars, an airplane propeller whizzing and half a dozen mechanics at work. Gleaming white hydroplanes, bobbing on the surface of the water.

The two young women and their uniformed escort saw none of these. Far, far above, like a winged insect, an airplane was circling. Higher and higher, it dipped and twisted and turned. Smaller and smaller, as though determined to efface itself completely.

"Look—oh, Corinne!"

The exclamation was short and sharp. The plane, somersaulting, seemed to catapult direct to earth. But now it was circling again, widening its arc, soaring smoothly.

"You see," Lieutenant Mustin explained to the young women beside him, "it may look dangerous to you, but it isn't really. People aren't used to the idea of flying, that's all. Why, Win's safer up there than he would be trying to cross a city street. That's one thing the war has done—and is doing. It's taught the world how important the airplane is—and how much more important it's going to be in the future. Some day everyone will be flying——"

The older of the two women interrupted. "He's coming down," she said. "And I'm glad! Henry, I don't think I want to see any more of this stunting, no matter how safe you say it is. I think Wallis and I will go home now. You can bring Lieutenant Spencer with you later."

* * * *

There came a day when Wallis Warfield's visit at Pensacola came to an end. It had been a pleasant visit —an introduction to a new sort of life. There was the excitement and electric quality in the air that attaches itself to a navy or army post. There were the young men who brashly risked their lives, and made sport of it. The parties. The good times. And the farewells——

Wallis had made many friends at Pensacola. Lieutenant Mustin was one of the most popular instructors at the aviation school. His wife was the younger sister of Mrs. George Barnett of Washington—Wallis' chaperon the night of her debut. And Corinne Mustin knew her young cousin well enough to guess why Wallis's color came so quickly those days, why her eyes seemed unusually bright, why she listened with quick interest for certain telephone calls and was indifferent to others.

Wallis had met many young officers at Pensacola. She had laughed and danced with them and accepted some of their invitations. But, most often, she accepted those of Lieutenant "Win" Spencer.

The day of farewell arrived at last. Wallis Warfield returned to her home in Baltimore. And letters followed swiftly.

There were letters postmarked "Pensacola, Fla." and addressed in a bold, masculine hand. Wallis wrote letters, too. She seemed less interested in the young Baltimoreans who had been her escorts before. She was usually at home when the postman arrived or, if she were not, was likely to telephone to know if anything had come addressed to her.

Romance? Infatuation? Love?

Nineteen-year-old Wallis Warfield did not know the difference, doubtless was scarcely aware that there was a difference. But handsome Lieutenant Spencer remained in her thoughts.

He came to Washington that summer while Wallis was visiting the Barnetts. The two were noticed together as an unusually attractive-looking couple—the dashing, debonair lieutenant and the smartly turned-out, vivacious debutante.

Lieutenant Spencer's leave ended and he returned to Pensacola. On Sept. 19, Mrs. John Freeman Raisin announced the engagement of her daughter, Wallis, to the Lieutenant. Baltimore newspapers reported the event thus:

"An engagement just announced of unusual interest to society in Maryland as well as in Virginia, is that of Miss Wallis Warfield, daughter of Mrs. John Freeman Raisin and the late Teackle Wallis Warfield, to Lieut. E. Winfield Spencer, Jr., U.S.N., of the Aviation Corps, son of Mr. and Mrs. E. Winfield Spencer of Highland Park, Chicago.

"The wedding will be one of the important events of November and will take place in the early part of the month.

"Miss Warfield has been one of the most popular girls in society since she made her debut two seasons ago and has been much entertained both here and in Washington where she has frequently visited her aunt, Mrs. D.

Buchanan Merryman. Miss Warfield, whose mother was before her marriage Miss Alice Montague, is related to distinguished Maryland and Virginia families. She is a granddaughter of the late Mr. and Mrs. Henry M. Warfield and niece of Mr. S. Davies Warfield of Baltimore.

"Lieutenant Spencer is a graduate of the U. S. Naval Academy and is now stationed at Pensacola, Fla., where he is one of the instructors in aviation."

A few days later the date of the wedding was announced, Nov. 8.

Such a short time and so much to crowd into it. Wallis and her mother planned the trousseau, shopped together, discussed the wedding arrangements. There were fittings at the dressmaker's for the bride and the six girls who were to be her bridesmaids. And there were friends who wanted to give parties and friends who sent wedding presents. And the telephone rang and the postman brought letters, and there were simply not enough hours in the daily cycle of 24 to do one-half of the things that should be done.

Presently the parties, honoring the bride-to-be, began.

Emily McLane Merryman gave a luncheon at "Gerar," her home near Cockeysville. Mrs. Aubrey Edmunds King gave another at the Baltimore Country Club. Mrs. Barnett and her daughter, Miss Leila Gordon, gave a tea dance at their home in Washington. Mrs. Henry C. Kirk, Jr., and her daughter, Miss Mary Kirk, gave a tea at the Baltimore Country Club. Lieutenant Spencer was host at a dinner at the Hotel Belvidere.

The ceremony took place at Christ Protestant Episcopal Church at 6:30 in the evening.

Tall white tapers burned before the altar, banked with annunciation lilies. Candles and white chrysanthemums decorated the church. Then, to the strains of organ music, the bridal procession moved down the aisle.

First the bridesmaids in gowns of orchid-colored faille and blue velvet, carrying yellow snapdragons and wearing blue velvet hats. They were: Miss Leila Gordon and Miss Mary Graham of Washington; Miss Ethel Spencer, sister of the bridegroom, of Chicago; Miss Emily Mc-Lane Merryman, Miss Mary Kirk, and Miss Mercer Taliaferro.

Then the matron of honor, Mrs. William B. Sturgis of New York, the former Miss Ellen Yuille of Baltimore, wearing a costume of Lucille blue with touches of silver and a blue satin hat with an orchid plume.

Then, on the arm of her uncle, S. Davies Warfield, came Wallis Warfield. She wore a gown of white panne velvet, embroidered with pearls and about her dark hair was a coronet of orange blossoms, from which fell a tulle veil. She carried a bouquet of white orchids and lilies of the valley.

Lieutenant Spencer, in full dress uniform, stood beside his best man, his brother, Dumaresque Spencer. The ushers, also in full dress naval uniforms, were: Lieut. Godfrey de Courcelles Chevalier; Lieut. Harold Perry Bartlett; Lieut. George Martin Cook; Lieut. John Homer Holt; and Lieut. De Witt Clinton Ramsey; and Kenneth Whiting.

The ceremony was read by the Rev. Edwin Barnes Niver. "Do you, Earl Winfield Spencer, take this woman to be your lawful wedded wife? . . . Do you, Bessie Wallis Warfield, take this man to be your lawful wedded husband . . ."

And so they were married——

Pictures, Inc.

Bigelow—International

Bigelow—International

PHOTOGRAPHIC STUDIES OF MRS. SIMPSON AS THE BRIDE OF LIEUTENANT E. WINFIELD SPENCER, U.S.N.

Chapter 6

❖

WAR TIMES IN FLORIDA AND CALIFORNIA
. . . SEPARATION

MRS. EARL WINFIELD SPENCER looked out over the bright strip of lawn, at the deep pink of the oleander blossoms across the way. A group of youngsters bareheaded and in light colored clothing, were romping in the next yard. Florida in January. Young Mrs. Spencer couldn't accept it—the vivid greenness and the flowers and the sky that was like that of mid-summer—as casually as everyone else seemed to. The letter in her hand said that the week before, in Baltimore, there had been snow.

The letter was from Mercer Taliaferro, one of the bridesmaids at the Spencers' wedding. Miss Taliaferro was coming to Florida for a visit. She was one of the girls Wallis Spencer had known since childhood. It would be grand, having her here in Pensacola. . . .

Lieutenant Spencer and his bride had come to Pensacola at the end of their honeymoon, spent at White Sulphur Springs. Lieutenant Spencer had to be back at his duties in the aviation school. Wallis was eager, too, to return to Florida. She had memories of Pensacola, as it had been the year before.

At first it had seemed the same. Parties, dinners, a

gay crowd dropping in informally . . . new officers and
their wives arriving . . . others going to far-away places
. . . more dances with young men in uniforms and more
pretty girls.

And yet there was a difference. It was apparent at
dinner tables, in the shops, in small groups and large
ones—everywhere one went. The war in Europe was
drawing closer. Men and women who had shaken their
heads complacently, sure that the horrors across the
Atlantic could never touch their own homes, were now
asking, "How long will it be? How long before America goes in?"

The talk was not of "preparedness" but "armed neu-
trality." Ex-president Taft and Dr. Nicholas Murray Butler and Ambassador Gerard made speeches. Rear Admiral Perry, addressing the convention of the National
Security League, urged the need of a big air fleet to
combat submarine warfare. Colonel Theodore Roosevelt endorsed a national military census. Congress was
wrangling over army and navy appropriation bills. Nine
states and the District of Columbia mobilized National
Guard Units. The *Lusitania* disaster—the German submarine blockade—"atrocities"—these were the phrases
heard on every side.

At Pensacola, Lieutenant "Win" Spencer and his
friends talked of the French war ace, Lieut. Guynemer,
and of the German, Lieut. von Richthofen who seemed to
be equal in the number of enemy planes each had
brought down—numbers that were incredible. They
talked, too, of the Lafayette Escadrille, American fliers
serving with the French forces, and called them "lucky"
to be seeing such action. And there was the rumor that
in England plans were underway to build 100 airplanes

capable of flying continuously for 10 hours. There was a report that a new "giant airplane" made in England had flown to a height of 7,000 feet, carrying 20 passengers.

America was awaking to the importance of the air. Rodman Wanamaker offered to supply funds to build an armed cruiser for the defense of New York City. An organization of patriotic women bought a Kite Balloon at the Pan-American Aeronautic Exposition and presented it to the army. Ruth Law won a trophy for record time in a flight from New York to Chicago. Ruth Law was recruiting aviators to join the army. A special commission reported to Congress on navy yards and navy stations, recommending the establishment of six aviation bases on the Pacific coast.

It was all disturbing, alarming, particularly to a girl who, only a few months before, had stood beside a young man in uniform and made her bridal vows. At parties the talk was gay and the laughter bright, but it was a gaiety, a brightness that masked something deeper.

How soon now? How soon before it came? Everyone asked the question.

Lieutenant Spencer and the other officers in the aviation school worked longer hours. It was a serious business, this getting ready for war. Rush orders came from Washington. The government needed aviators. The government needed more planes, too—of new design. Planes that could fly longer and carry heavier guns and shoot with more deadly aim.

The Military Training Camp Association sent a telegram to Secretary Newton D. Baker, offering the services of men trained at Plattsburg and other camps to the nation "in the crisis." Mass meetings were held in Philadelphia and Boston and Chicago and Sheboygan, Wis., and Norfolk, Va. "Pilgrims of Patriotism" set out for a giant demonstration in Washington.

And on April 6, at his desk in the White House, President Wilson wrote his name across an official document.

It was war——

*   *   *   *

Lieutenant and Mrs. E. Winfield Spencer decided, immediately upon arriving at San Diego, Cal., that they were going to like it. They did. Mrs. Spencer liked the little flat she found and Lieutenant Spencer, impatient over delay at getting into service in France, knew that, here in California, he was doing a job that was more important.

The United States faced a shocking lack of aviators to fly the planes that were being built. Recruits poured into army and navy camps in every state. Flags were flying, bands playing, men marching. But they were untrained men, the raw stuff of which armed forces are made.

Lieutenant Spencer had no time now for parties or dancing or bridge playing. Everything was feverish rush and excitement and haste in the air corps. Everything to be done at once. So few to do it.

Wallis Spencer, left to herself, made friends—as she has always, wherever she has been. Rear Admiral Fullam was stationed at San Diego, and his daughters, Miss Rhoda Fullam and Mrs. Austin Sands, met young Mrs. Spencer. They found that, in Washington, they had mutual friends. Soon the three were together frequently, almost inseparable.

Years later when Wallis Spencer had put California behind her forever she paid tribute to that land of sunshine and orange groves and florid beauty. Holding up a pin which contained a large diamond, she said to a friend:

"Look—I have this. Some day when I just can't stand it to be away any longer, I'll sell it and go to California."

From San Diego, Wallis Spencer wrote to friends in Baltimore about the glorious California climate, about the new friends she had made, the places to which she had gone and was going. Other things she left unsaid. She has never been one to air domestic affairs, but the truth is that things were not going well with the Spencers.

There were differences—frequently. There were scenes which, doubtless, today neither of the principals wishes to recall. Gradually, though, each came to realize the truth. It had been a marriage that was youthful, impetuous, based on short acquaintance instead of deep-seated devotion. There had been the dazzle of romantic surroundings. There had been the excitement of pre-war days. And it had been a mistake.

The realization came slowly, painfully. They knew it before the war days came to an end. They knew it before that insane, exultant Armistice Day of Nov. 11, 1918, when all America danced in the streets and screamed joyously and caught strangers in their arms and hurled ticker tape and found none of these things sufficient to express its transcendent joy.

Peace and the war over and the boys coming home from France! Peace for America—peace for the World!

*   *   *   *

When Lieutenant Spencer was ordered to Washington, D.C., he and his wife both thought that the change, perhaps, might mean a new start. Wallis was anxious to see her mother again, her aunts and cousins in Washington. Perhaps, there, she and "Win" would find some of the happiness together that they had known during his visit the summer before their marriage. Perhaps they could leave the past behind——

They said farewell to California and arrived in Washington. Later it was Lieutenant Spencer who departed, alone. He was ordered to sail for Shanghai. Wallis remained in Washington and their farewell had the solemnity with which men and women face important decisions in their lives. It was, each believed, a farewell that was to be permanent.

Presently, as the days passed, Wallis Spencer began to pick up the threads of her life before her marriage. Her mother was living at Chevy Chase, Md., where she was hostess and manager of the Chevy Chase Club. Wallis saw her aunt, Mrs. D. Buchanan Merryman, frequently and visited the Barnetts at their country estate, "Wakefield Manor".

Rhoda Fullam and her sister, Marianna Sands, were back in Washington, and at their home Wallis Spencer's circle of friends was considerably widened. She met the younger members of the army and navy set and the diplomatic corps. She began to be seen about at dinner parties, at teas and receptions at the Embassies and Legations.

It was the time when the "Soixante Gourmets" held a prominent place in Washington social life. The "Soixante Gourmets" was a luncheon club, composed of 60 of the younger foreign diplomats—the chargés d'affaires and secretaries from the various foreign offices—who met each mid-day at the Hotel Hamilton. Each member was expected to bring a woman guest, and a huge table, extending entirely down one side of the dining room, was reserved for the club.

The talk at "Soixante Gourmets" luncheons invariably was lively and entertaining, conducted in three or four languages—French, Spanish, Italian—all within earshot. A young woman fortunate enough to be a guest might find herself seated with young Baron von Plessen on one side and Don Gelasio Caetani, Italian ambassador, nearby. Across the table might be Pete de Sibour, one of the founders of the club, and Jules Henry of the French foreign office. Harold Sims of the British Embassy was almost sure to be present. So was Felipe A. Espil, today the Argentine Ambassador.

Wallis Spencer appeared at "Soixante Gourmets" luncheons frequently. She was often seen, too, with Mr. and Mrs. Frederick Neilson. For a time when the Neilsons left Washington to return to their home in New York, Wallis Spencer took their apartment. The Neilsons' friends thought it amusing that so many people made comments on the fact that "Freddy" looked so very much like the Prince of Wales. The resemblance, as a matter of fact, was striking.

In Washington, too, began Wallis Spencer's friendship with Ethel Noyes, daughter of Frank B. Noyes, president of the Associated Press, and sister of Frances Noyes Hart, the author. Ethel Noyes married Willmott Lewis, later knighted by King George V, and she is known today, both in America and Europe, for her wit. No beauty, out-spoken, Lady Lewis said of the honors conferred upon her husband, "Well, it took King George to make a lady of me!"

Wallis Spencer and her friends frequently were guests

at dinner at the home of Harold Sims, who, a bachelor, had an imposing house and gave many large parties. His reputation as a host was enhanced by the presence of an ultra-English butler, Jones, about whom stories are still current in Washington. Harold Sims' home was one in which lady guests were never served any beverage stronger than wine. He disapproved of women drinking cocktails and highballs and, while the grog tray was brought about for the men, the ladies sipped their Barsac and water.

For a time Wallis Spencer shared a home in Georgetown with Mrs. Luke McNamee, whose husband, absent on duty, was chief of the naval intelligence office. Later Captain McNamee was naval attaché of the American Embassy in London, and still later, as Rear Admiral McNamee, was ordered home to command the destroyer squadron of the battle fleet on the Pacific. For several years he was president of the War College at Newport, R.I., resigning in 1934 to become chairman of the International Telephone and Telegraph Corporation. Mrs. McNamee, daughter of Admiral Swinburn, is well known for her portrait paintings of children.

The little house where Wallis Spencer and Dorothy McNamee lived in in Georgetown was unimpressive, viewed from the street. Inside it was charming. Here, informally but attractively, the great names of Washington society were entertained. Here there was sure to be sprightly conversation of all that was new in politics and art and literature and events of the day, both at home and abroad.

In 1923 Wallis Spencer made her first trip to Europe. She went with numerous letters of introduction, and in Paris joined Ethel Noyes. On her return from this trip,

Wallis Spencer announced a decision. Lieutenant Spencer was still stationed at Shanghai. Wallis had made up her mind to join him and seek a reconciliation.

Her mother, married for the third time and now Mrs. Charles Gordon Allen of Washington, dreaded to see her daughter go. She said to a friend, "It's such a long way and such a strange place—Shanghai. But I've always let Wallis make her own decisions and I'm not going to try to influence her now. I wouldn't want her to stay because she thought I wanted her to. She mustn't know how I feel about it—but I'm afraid for her. And I'm afraid no good will come of this trip."

But Wallis had made up her mind to go to China. And so bags were packed and tickets purchased and, amid farewells and with characteristic composure, Wallis Spencer set off for the ancient Land of the Manchus.

It was the beginning of a new chapter in her life.

Chapter 7

❖

A TALE OF TWO CITIES

THE years 1925 and 1926 in Wallis Spencer's life were a tale of two cities. Cities as unlike as any two on this earth—Shanghai, China, and Warrenton, Va.

Shanghai, the oriental seaport, with its million and a half population, its teeming harbor, its astounding mixture of poverty and opulence, of ancient civilization and modern commerce, of Buddhist temples and Hollywood motion pictures, "the most cosmopolitan city in the world."

Warrenton, where 1,450 souls, comprising the population, go their pleasant, prosaic way, farming fertile fields set amid rolling hills, riding and hunting in season, and giving little thought to the rest of the world.

Shanghai and Warrenton—

Wallis Spencer knew them both, and made a place for herself in each.

* * * *

In Shanghai, Lieutenant and Mrs. Spencer were entertained a good deal. The army and navy set gave parties. There were luncheons and teas and sight-seeing trips. The Spencers took an attractive flat and, from her maid, Wallis learned to speak a few Chinese phrases—enough to make shopping easier and to give directions when she rode in rikshas.

And, for a time, it seemed that the purpose of her trip had been accomplished. There is no doubt that the lieutenant and his wife both made sincere efforts to patch up the raveled course of their domestic life. Older, wiser, they did try—both of them—to avoid the mistakes of the past.

Lieutenant Spencer was obliged to be away much of the time. When some new friends, Mr. and Mrs. Herman Rogers, asked Wallis to visit them in Peiping, she accepted the invitation. The Rogers are Americans who spend their time in whatever part of the globe seems most attractive. Their friendship with Wallis Spencer has continued through the years. They were to meet later on the French Riviera. Still later—in September, 1936—when King Edward VIII, returning from his summer cruise on the "Nahlin", entertained a group of friends at Balmoral Castle, the names of his guests were flashed around the world by news services. The list included—besides the King's brothers, the Duke of York and the Duke of Kent, and their wives, the Duchess of York and the Duchess of Kent, and other titled guests—Mrs. Ernest Simpson, the former Wallis Spencer, and Mr. and Mrs. Herman Rogers.

That visit in Peiping was a pleasant one. At the American Embassy there were friends Wallis Spencer had known in Washington, others with whom she had mutual acquaintances. She went to "at homes" in Chinese gardens that looked like picture postcards, to Legation receptions where Japanese, German, Scandinavian and Italian ministers and attachés bowed and paid courtly compliments and sandalled servants passed trays of food. The

Rogers took their guest to visit ancient temples and palaces, to the cinema that, in Peiping, is as important as the opera or theater, to shop in the "silk street" and "jade street".

The influence of that year in China was to stamp itself indelibly on Wallis Spencer. An indication of this is the famous photographic portrait of her made by Man Ray, the French artist. In this photograph, she wears a coat of Chinese cut. She is standing against a dark background and her face, turned slightly, has the dignity and fragility of a Chinese princess, pictured on a priceless bit of porcelain.

Today, in her London home, there are numerous reminders of her stay in China. There is a handsome screen, standing in the entrance hall, and, in the drawing room, two beautiful porcelain fishes. There are lacquer and porcelain boxes and bits of brocade. In China, too, Wallis Spencer began her collection of "lucky" elephants—tiny figures carved of ivory and jade and turquoise and a dozen other substances. Her favorite colors are the Chinese shades—unusual blues, jade, amber, soft browns, flame and the pink of rose quartz.

From Peiping Wallis Spencer returned to Shanghai, and the months drifted on. At the end of a year she and Lieutenant Spencer faced the conclusion that was inevitable. They decided that, for each, it was best to end their marriage.

They said farewells, knowing that, this time, they were to be final, and Wallis sailed for America.

*   *   *   *

The Warren Green Hotel in Warrenton, Va., is a rambling structure where life moves complacently, seldom with needless energy. From its windows, there is a view of Warrenton's two principal thoroughfares, and, beyond, the rolling Virginia landscape.

Wallis Spencer arrived there June 10, 1926. A year later she said, in answer to questioning by Judge George Latham Fletcher, "I came to Warrenton to be near my family. I knew some people here. All my family are in Washington."

At the Warren Green Hotel she unpacked her trunks with their steamer labels. She took out her screens and brocades and lacquer boxes. Presently—she has a decided talent for making her surroundings reflect her personality—the two-room suite became colorful and homelike. Visitors who were entertained in that living room remember that there were always flowers in profusion. They remember the display of "lucky" elephants —and some of them added to the collection.

Wallis Spencer had no servants at the Warren Green Hotel, but Jake, the grizzled old colored porter, could not do enough for her. Jake used to wash her dog, "Sandy". "Sandy" had been acquired by adoption and had other owners, but as long as Wallis Spencer was in Warrenton, he remained with her.

Warrenton is in a section of Virginia where there are many country estates, where hunting and racing are subjects of the keenest interest and several families own their own packs of hounds. Each year the outstanding event is the Warrenton Gold Cup Race in which gentlemen jockeys from all over the country ride.

The day starts with luncheon at one of the large country homes. House and gardens and grounds are always overflowing with guests. Then there is the race, laid out over a course crossing "Clovelly", the home of Mr. and

Mrs. Baldwin Spilman, who keep open house for the day. At night there is the dance at the Warrenton Country Club at which the men wear the pink coats of the hunt and the women their smartest formal gowns.

Wallis Spencer soon found herself very much at home in this life. Among her friends were Mr. and Mrs. Fred Hasrick and Mr. and Mrs. Sterling Larrabee. Occasionally she drove over to Middleburg to visit Mr. and Mrs. Arthur White. She was friendly, too, with Mr. and Mrs. Robert Winmill and Mr. and Mrs. John Buchanan.

She made a trip to New York that year—a casual visit that was unimportant except for a single event. She went to dinner at the home of an old friend, Mrs. Jacques Raffray who, as Mary Kirk, had been one of the bridesmaids at the Spencers' marriage. Two of the other guests that evening were Mr. and Mrs. Ernest Simpson. Ernest Simpson, a tall, well-set-up man with English coloring— blue eyes, light brown hair and mustache—was employed by the ship-chartering firm of which his father was a member. Mrs. Simpson, the former Mrs. Dorothea Parsons Dechert, was the daughter of Arthur Webb Parsons and a great granddaughter of a former Chief Justice of Massachusetts. The Simpsons had been married in 1923 and had a daughter.

Wallis Spencer saw the Simpsons once or twice after that. She met a number of other people in New York, did some shopping, saw some plays, and returned to Warrenton.

She had not intended, when she went to the little Virginia town, to make it her permanent residence. But she enjoyed it there. She found she liked it better the longer she stayed. Frequently she saw her old friends from Baltimore and Washington.

She went to Baltimore for the Maryland Hunt Cup Race, joining a group of friends from Pittsburgh. One of them was Elizabeth Key Lloyd, now Mrs. Morgan Schiller, and later the group drove to Wye House on the Eastern Shore, owned by the Lloyd family.

Wye House is a famous pre-Revolutionary country house. The original house, built in the seventeenth century, was burned and rebuilt before the Revolution. Some of the smaller buildings, still standing, are of seventeenth century construction. The orangery, back of the house, is said to be one of the finest examples of Georgian architecture in America. Wye House is famous, too, for its box hedge labyrinth. All of the furnishings in the house are original colonial pieces, and lighting, by night, is by means of lamps and candles.

The place abounds in traditions and has rooms that are believed to be haunted. There was a good deal of discussion, on Wallis Spencer's visit to Wye House, about the "haunted" rooms and who should be assigned to them. The week-end passed, however, without ghostly visitations.

On Oct. 25, 1927, S. Davies Warfield died in Baltimore. His niece attended the funeral, Oct. 27, at Emanuel Protestant church. It was at three o'clock in the afternoon and at that time all trains of the Seaboard Air Line railroad were stopped for a period of five minutes.

On Dec. 6, in the Circuit Court of Fauquier County, at Warrenton, the hearing of Wallis Spencer's divorce suit began. Judge George Latham Fletcher presided. The charge was desertion and, on Dec. 10, the decree was granted.

Wallis Spencer left that courtroom in Warrenton free of marital bonds. It was the ending of one chapter in her life. . . . A chapter that had stretched from Baltimore to Florida and California and Washington and Paris and Shanghai. . . . It was the beginning of a new chapter . . . and even Wallis Simpson scarcely could have dreamed what distances this new one was to take her.

Chapter 8

❖

REMARRIAGE . . . LIFE IN LONDON

LATE afternoon lights glowed in the New York apartment living room. There was a fire burning on the grate and a tray on the low table before the davenport. Ice tinkled in glasses and twisted spirals of cigarette smoke rose, blending with the scent of roses in a silver bowl against the wall.

Two women and a man sat near the fire. Others, across the room, were looking out at the Manhattan skyline, beginning to sparkle, here and there, with its nightly radiance.

The low hum of voices was interrupted by a man standing before the fireplace.

"But there's a fortune in it!" he exclaimed. "It's the biggest thing in years——"

"What is, Morgan?" one of the women at the window demanded.

"Why, this thing I've been telling you about. These construction elevators. I've gone over the whole proposition. It's sound—absolutely 100 per cent!"

Another voice, not loud but receiving instant attention, spoke then. It was a woman's voice.

"Why, that's marvelous!" she said. "Here you have this new business you're so enthusiastic about and here

79

am I, wanting a job. There must be something in such a big business that I could do."

"You—a job?"

"Why, Wallis!"

There were other protests. "What on earth do you want a job for?" "What could you do?" "Honestly I never *heard* of such a thing!"

"Do you really mean it, Wallis?" the man asked doubtfully.

"Certainly I mean it. Why not?"

"By George, I believe you do!" The man before the fireplace turned, studied the face of the woman who had spoken. "You could do it, too!" he announced, snapping his fingers. "By George—of course you could. You've got personality, appearance, enthusiasm!"

"But she's never done anything like that in her life," said one of the others, coming forward. "Wallis—you can't be serious. You don't mean that you really want to go to work!"

Wallis Spencer smiled. "Other people get jobs, don't they?" she said. "Then, why can't I? I do want a job; it's the one thing I do want."

The man beside her took out a cigarette case, offered it and struck a match.

"You'd be splendid at any job you made up your mind to undertake," he said quietly, "but somehow I can't think of you in connection with anything as ponderous and ugly as construction elevators. What do you plan to do about them? Demonstrate them——?"

"She could sell them!" the other man cut in abruptly. "It's a great idea. Why, Wallis could hypnotize anyone into buying anything in the world. Maybe she hasn't had business experience, but she won't need that. Wallis, it's

MRS. SIMPSON, WHEN SHE AND HER HUSBAND, E. WINFIELD
SPENCER, LIVED AT SAN DIEGO, CALIF.

a great idea. It's better than that; it's brilliant. I want you to come out to Pittsburgh and talk this over. We're going to go through with it!"

*　　　*　　　*　　　*

Wallis Spencer made the trip to Pittsburgh, but she did not sell even one construction elevator. Later judgment prevailed and she gave up the venture.

Perhaps, as a business woman, she would have made a success—even in such an unusual field. After all, it was her grandfather, Henry M. Warfield, who persuaded directors of the Baltimore and Ohio railroad to build their first grain elevator, said to be the first one in the country. The episode is interesting because it is one more adding insight into the character of this unusual woman.

*　　　*　　　*　　　*

Warrenton, Va., was a place of peace and comfort and friends, but presently Wallis Spencer felt once more the urge to travel. Her aunt, Mrs. D. Buchanan Merryman, agreed to go with her to Europe.

So again bags were packed and tickets bought. Again there were farewells waved from the deck of an ocean liner. And again Wallis Spencer was on her way to new adventures.

She and Mrs. Merryman spent some time in Paris and in the south of France. And then they went to London, where, shortly after their arrival, they encountered Ernest Simpson.

He was, by this time, living in London. Separated and then divorced from his wife, he had gone to London as attorney for the ship-chartering firm of Simpson and Simpson in which today he is a partner. It was natural for Ernest Simpson to feel at home in England. Though he was born in New York City, his father, Ernest L. Simpson of New York, was born a British subject. Ernest Simpson's sister, Lady Carr-Smiley, had chosen a British husband and had lived in London for several years. He himself, as an undergraduate at Harvard, had left the university early in 1918 to enlist in the British Cold-stream Guards—which happens to be King Edward VIII's regiment. Six months after enlistment Ernest Simpson received a second lieutenant's commission. At the end of the war he returned to the United States, took up his studies again at Harvard and was graduated.

Those who know Ernest Simpson well invariably speak first of his appearance. He is tall, rather blond, with a pink and white freshness of complexion. He has squarely set shoulders, a distinguished manner and a conservative taste in clothes. One of his hobbies is collecting old books, and he is proud of his collection. History interests him. So does biography. He likes travel, too, and has a great fund of knowledge about the places where he has been.

As a host he is easy to talk to and entertaining. He played host to Wallis Simpson and her aunt frequently that winter in London. He took them to smart restaurants, to the theater, to Covent Garden. They met many of his friends. He sent flowers. He paid subtle compliments and, with a hundred little attentions, made it plain to Wallis Simpson how much he admired her.

It was a courtship unlike any she had known before. She admired Ernest Simpson, enjoyed his companionship. In his presence she felt security and a stability that was new—and stability was a quality in which Wallis Spencer's life had been lacking. There had been gaiety, glamour and excitement, but these can lose value. Strong,

dependable and gallant, Ernest Simpson pled his case—
and won.

From Baltimore, on an August day in 1918, came the
news:

"Mrs. Warfield Spencer, daughter of Mrs. Charles
Gordon Allen of Washington, and Mr. Ernest Simpson
of London, England, were married Saturday, July 21, in
London, according to announcement made by Mr. and
Mrs. Allen."

The marriage ceremony was the simplest, followed by
a wedding trip to Spain and the Balearic Islands.

Back in London, Mr. and Mrs. Simpson first lived at
Grosvenor House. Then they moved to 12 Upper Berkeley Street—a house owned by Lady Chatham. It was a
small place, but attractively furnished, with pine-pan-
nelled walls, bright chintz hangings and gleaming old
silver. And, of course, Wallis made it home-like with
flowers—quantities of them at all times.

But Wallis Simpson missed her friends in Virginia
and Maryland. For months she was home-sick and for
months the English ways of doing things—such simple
things as shopping and giving orders to servants and having tea in the morning instead of coffee—seemed strange
and unnatural. She discovered how very, very different,
despite the bond of a common language, is life in England and America.

A little over a year after her marriage came news that
brought her back to America on the first liner. Her
mother was ill in Washington. Seriously ill. When the
daughter reached her mother's bedside, Mrs. Allen was
unconscious. She never regained consciousness, though
she lived for a week.

The death of her mother was the greatest sadness Wallis Simpson had ever known. Such loyalty and devotion as existed between these two is rare. Wholeheartedly, unselfishly the mother had made her daughter's welfare the single aim of her life. It was a deep-seated affection that was returned. Today the high place Wallis Simpson occupies in the world, the honors that have come to her are a tribute to that mother's memory.

When Mrs. Simpson returned to London the sadness went with her. She was in mourning, saw very few of her friends. The foreignness of the city seemed more pronounced than ever. More than ever, she missed the friends and relatives she had left behind in America.

Gradually the unhappy months passed. Gradually the sense of loneliness slipped away. Mr. and Mrs. Simpson made some acquaintances at the American Embassy. Presently they were receiving invitations, entertaining in turn.

They met Mr. and Mrs. Benjamin Thaw. Mrs. Thaw is the sister of Lady Furness and Mrs. Gloria Vanderbilt, and her husband, a brother of Colonel Thaw who organized the Lafayette Escadrille, was first secretary of the Embassy. They met Lord and Lady Furness and Mrs. Vanderbilt. They attended parties given by Captain Galbraith, naval attaché at the American Embassy, and his wife. The Galbraiths' entertainments were famous in London for their lavishness.

It was not long before the Simpsons' circle of friends increased. It included Mr. and Mrs. Reginald Foster. Others were Vincent Massey, the Canadian minister, and his wife, and Vincent Massey's brother, Raymond Massey, the actor, and his wife.

Mr. and Mrs. Simpson entertained a good deal in a

very inconspicuous way. Lady and Sir Willmott Lewis
were among their guests frequently. Frances Noyes
Hart, visiting her sister, came, too. Mrs. Erskine Gwinne
was another American friend.

In 1929 the Simpsons moved from the house on Upper Berkeley Street to an apartment on Bryanston Court.
That apartment was dignified without being pretentious,
comfortable and homelike. It was decorated by a swank
London firm, but Mrs. Simpson chose the colors used
in her rooms and the result was a tribute to her infallible
taste.

The walls of the living room were a pale antique chartreuse, with curtains of the same hue at the windows.
Tall crystal vases, usually filled with flame-colored flowers, added a brilliant accent. There was a mantel and,
over it, a huge mirror. Book shelves, for Ernest Simpson's prized volumes, lined the walls. There were plenty
of comfortable chairs, grouped to make conversation easy.
Plenty of little tables displaying Wallis Simpson's bright
Chinese lacquer boxes.

The dining room was a small one—or considered so in
London. Dominating the room was the mirror-topped
table, large enough to seat 12 or 14 guests. Mrs. Simpson likes this table because she thinks it contributes to the
gaiety of meals. The mirror top is left uncovered at dinner. At luncheon, instead of linen, bright-colored flower
prints, mounted, serve as place mats.

To operate this household Mrs. Simpson employed a
cook and kitchen maid, parlor maid and chamber maid
as well as her personal maid. She is exacting with servants but they are loyal, invariably remaining with her
for years. Kane, the Scotch parlor maid, has held her post

for a long period. Mrs. Rolph, the cook, has been employed for four years.

Mrs. Rolph, besides being an excellent cook, happens to be the wife of a sailor serving on Lord Louis Mountbatten's ship. When the ship is in port, Mrs. Simpson does no entertaining.

"You see, I have no cook!" she explains.

By June, 1931, Wallis Simpson was happy and contented in London. She had friends of whom she was fond, an attractive home and life had settled into a pleasant, if rather routine pattern.

Many of the women she knew had been presented at Court. They thought that Wallis should be, too.

She showed little interest in the suggestion.

"But you should. Really you should!" the others insisted.

Wallis couldn't see that being presented at Court could make any difference in her life. Things were going along well enough as they were. There wasn't anyone she wanted to impress and she wasn't a social climber. Why should she don plumes and a court train and set off for the palace?

At last, though, she was persuaded. "Very well," she said, "I'll do it if it doesn't cost anything."

And she did. From one friend she borrowed the gown with the court train and from another the three white plumes for her hair. She bought a band of aquamarines to hold the plumes in place and then—at the last minute —saw a beautiful aquamarine cross. It was four inches long and made of gorgeous stones, and Wallis has a weakness for aquamarines. She bought it, spending more than she might have on an entire court costume, and wore the cross suspended from a cord about her throat, with her borrowed finery.

The presentation took place June 10, 1931. It was the fourth and final court of the season. Besides King George and Queen Mary, the Prince of Wales, the Duke of Gloucester, and Prince George were present. Other members of the royal family attending were Princess Mary, the Countess of Harewood, and her husband, the Earl of Harewood; the Duke of Connaught; Princess Alice, Countess of Athlone and Major General the Earl of Athlone, and Lady Louis Mountbatten.

Mrs. Charles G. Dawes, wife of the American ambassador, presented nine American women. They were: Mrs. William R. Amon of New York, daughter of the U. S. Consul General in London; Mrs. Quentell Violett of New York; Miss Carol Donohugh of New York; Mrs. James Gaylord Baldwin, 2nd, portrait painter and member of the Columbus, Ohio, Junior League; Mrs. Charles O. Broy, of Sperryville, Va.; Mrs. Herbert C. Greer of Morgantown, W. Va.; Mrs. Ernest L. Ives of Bloomington, Ill.; Miss Barbara Peart of San Francisco, Cal.; and Miss Augusta Trimble of Seattle, Wash.

A news correspondent wrote of the occasion:

"As the presentees moved through the corridors of Buckingham Palace toward the scarlet and gold stateroom, they were entertained by the strains of soft music from a concealed orchestra. On all sides were high banks of roses and hydrangeas.

"The King and Queen, accompanied by other members of the royal family, entered the throne room at half past nine o'clock. The Prince of Wales, absent the night before, took his place behind the golden throne of his father and mother."

This was the scene as, one by one, the women to be presented went forward to make their bows. All in their handsomest gowns and most glittering jewels. Assembled in the impressive gathering were Indian princes and their Maharanees, ambassadors and their ladies, each in court costume, from France, Brazil, Portugal, Italy, Belgium, Japan, Poland, Chile, Russia, the Netherlands—and a dozen other countries. A ceremony that was colorful, solemn and dignified in the extreme.

Later, when the presentation was over, Mr. and Mrs. Simpson went to the party given by Lady Furness. There, too, was H.R.H., the Prince of Wales. Mrs. Simpson made another curtsy, this time to the Prince.

It was—at least, it may have been—a night to make history.

Chapter 9

❖

PORTRAIT OF WALLIS SIMPSON

COLUMNS have been written about Mrs. Ernest Simpson's gowns, her furs and her jewels.

She is, as she has been described, one of the best dressed women in the world. Usually the gowns she buys in Paris are designed by Mainbocher. Some have been by Molyneux. She does not, contrary to reports, like to wear black, but did last year, in accord with all the fashionable world of England, in mourning for King George.

Blue is her color—particularly in off-shades that are unusually becoming, with her blue eyes, creamy skin and rich brown hair. She likes to tan in summer, but avoids letting her skin brown deeply.

Her smile is flashing, brilliant, revealing extraordinarily white teeth.

She does not affect dark nail polish, preferring a pale pink shade.

As a young girl, the despair of her life was the fact that her waistline was so small. Today Parisian designers agree that Mrs. Simpson's figure is close to perfection. It is a figure that sets off the crisp, trim sport clothes she likes to wear.

She wears beautifully cut, tailored suits in quiet shades very often—usually with bright blouses. Last summer one of her favorite outfits was such a suit, worn with a satin blouse in jockey colors, made with the colors alternating, as in a jockey's shirt.

Day-time clothes designed for Mrs. Simpson invariably are cut high at the throat and have long, tight sleeves. Her evening gowns, in contrast, are very formal.

She is one of the few women in the world to whom backless evening gowns are becoming. Her taste, however, does not run to extremes.

Purple, the shade of royalty, is unusually becoming to Mrs. Simpson. She has a purple and black sport costume, and with it, to hold her hair in place when she goes hatless, wears a band of purple ribbons, woven and fastened about her head like a coronet braid. Her maid makes these bands and she has them in many colors.

The only "frou-frou" costume she ever owned was one in her summer wardrobe. It was a black crepe evening gown, severely plain in front, with many, many tiny ruffles at the back, each edged with white, and spreading like a peacock's plumage. Another black evening gown of classic lines has bands of bead embroidery in vivid shades.

She owns a coat of sables and one of mink. She does not wear silver fox or other "furry" furs. The sable and mink coats are from Revillon's in London. She likes American shoes, usually made by Delman. Antoine de Paris is her hair-dresser.

*   *   *   *

But it is Wallis Simpson's jewels that cause other women to sigh with envy!

Photographs showing her wearing pearls may be

classed invariably as dating from years ago. She no longer cares for pearls and never wears them.

She does wear rubies, sapphires, aquamarines, emeralds, diamonds. With sport clothes, frequently she wears a triangular-shaped clip with sides about two-and-a-half inches long and covered with small square stones of myriad hues.

Her daytime jewelry includes a necklace of baguette diamonds, set vertically instead of horizontally. At the centers of the front and sides are large emeralds. With the necklace she wears a ring, set with a three-cornered emerald and three-cornered diamond.

She has beautiful diamond clips which she wears also in the daytime, and a diamond bracelet in the shape of a cord, with a square of platinum and diamonds on one side which, studied closely, reveals the face of a watch.

Once she disliked earrings; now she wears them frequently. Her favorites are a pair made like sprays of flowers. The minute blossoms are set with beautifully-cut sapphires and the leaves and stems are of diamonds.

For evening she has complete sets of emeralds, of sapphires, of rubies and of aquamarines. They are in modern settings of unusual design. Most of them have been made by the Paris jewelers, Van Cleef and Arpels.

*   *   *   *

But other women have jewels. Other women have beautiful gowns. What are the qualities which have won for Wallis Simpson the place she holds in the world today?

Charm?

Yes, decidedly. The charm of a controlled, sophisticated woman, quick to sympathize and quick to understand the problems of others. Tactful in the extreme. Says a close friend:

"Wallis has an amazing ability to keep her opinions to herself. If she thinks an acquaintance is doing something that is unwise, that something about another person's life might be remedied or changed for the better, she is likely to suggest, in the mildest way, that such a change might be a good thing. She can do more with suggestions than others who are emphatic in their comments."

The character of such a woman is not easy to express.

There is the surface glamour—her beauty, her wit, the sparkle of an alert personality who has been in many of the interesting places of the world and known many of its most interesting men and women.

But there is much that is deeper in Mrs. Simpson's nature. Loyalty. Self-discipline. Courage. Complete honesty and complete lack of pretense. An unusual gift of analysis and unusual ability to come to sound decisions. She has the widest interests—art and literature and events of state, as well as the theater and racing at Ascot and Aintree. Her absorbing interest, though, is in other people, and her judgment of others is almost unerring.

*   *   *   *

The world knows Wallis Simpson in headlines; the world does not know, however, such facts as these:

She likes motion picture comedies—particularly those made by Eddie Cantor and Harold Lloyd.

She is very undemonstrative.

She is friendly, but has what has been described as "a wonderful way of keeping people at a distance."

She can complete a jigsaw puzzle in half the time the average person takes.

She has a photographic mind and, having entered a room, can step outside and relate in detail exactly what that room contained. Friends tell the story of a time when Mrs. Simpson and several others went to visit a famous cathedral. They gazed, impressed, at lofty Gothic arches, at the beautiful altar and richly colored windows and stone floors hallowed by years and the tread of reverent feet. Then, leaving the cathedral behind, they stepped out into the daylight.

Said Wallis Simpson, "What did you think of the clock?"

Clock? Immediately there were exclamations. None of the others in the group had seen a clock. They declared that Wallis certainly must be mistaken.

She smiled and said, "Let's look again."

Back into the cathedral they went, and down a corridor. There—sure enough—in a design on the wall was a clock. It was ancient as its surroundings, in dull colors and rather unusual. But a clock, nevertheless.

To picture Wallis Simpson, though, it is necessary to see her in her home, as guests do of an afternoon when they drop in for tea. Such informal "at homes" take place three or four times each week.

The hour is five o'clock. The drawing room, with its furnishings of rich and unobtrusive tones, dark polished wood and masses of vivid, exotic blossoms, is softly lighted. Groups of men and women—eight or ten of them—are talking. Now and then a ripple of laughter rises.

Mrs. Simpson, in a gown of blue set off by the gleam of diamonds, sits before a low table on which are arranged silver and crystal and china. She serves her guests, stopping to greet new arrivals, to join in the talk, telling an anecdote or listening to one.

"Slipper," the Cairn terrier, dozes on the floor at a distance. The parlor maid enters with a square silver box, with shelves holding canapés and, after the guests have helped themselves, places it near the fire to keep the canapés warm. There will be, too, on a tray, a fresh loaf of brownly crusted bread, potted shrimps and lettuce. Such foods are more to Mrs. Simpson's taste, personally, than elaborate ones or sweets.

Guests come and go. Lady Oxford, whose books, a dozen years ago, were considered rather daring and who has lectured in America, may be there. In London where, should the King be present, ladies curtsy before His Majesty immediately upon entering a room, Lady Oxford is famous for her curtsy. She is said, in fact, to make the most graceful curtsy of anyone in London.

Perhaps, as the tea hour continues, the Duke and Duchess of Sutherland may arrive. Or Lady Honor and Mr. Henry Channon. Later, or on another day, the guests may include Lord and Lady Brownlow, Mr. and Mrs. Colin Buist, Harold Nicholson, M.P., Lord Berners, Lady Diana Duff-Cooper, John Gunther, the European news correspondent, Lord and Lady Louis Mountbatten, Lady Cunard, widow of Sir Bache Cunard, and Lady Colfax.

Lady Cunard and Lady Colfax are both renowned London hostesses. So is Lady Oxford. There was an evening within the past year when all three were guests at a dinner party given by Mrs. Simpson. The wit and brilliance of that dinner party is still discussed. The three famous ladies held forth in lively fashion. The three

MRS. SIMPSON
DRESSED FOR THE PRESENTATION AT COURT

famous ladies told anecdotes and exchanged quips and sparkled.

Another at that dinner party was Alexander Woollcott. He, like the others about the table, listened, saying less and less. Lady Cunard and Lady Oxford and Lady Colfax talked on; the silence of the others deepened.

Presently, out of the silence, Mr. Woollcott spoke. Looking down at the plate of lobster mousse that had been set before him, he said in precise, clipped tones:

"Never before have I been served peach ice cream at this time in a meal."

*   *   *   *

Those who envy Wallis Simpson her success as a hostess may be guided by some of these hints.

She feels it is important at dinner parties to keep the conversation, at least more or less, general. For this reason, she does not like large groups.

She believes a good hostess is one who is able to throw the ball of conversation, seeing to it that every one is included.

She thinks, too, that:

Food should be perfect (as it invariably is in her home) but too much makes people dull and uninteresting. Cooking that is excellent, but of rather simple form, is likely to please guests more than elaborate dishes.

Alcoholic drinks—at least more than two before dinner—dull both the appetite and the wit.

A wise hostess never entertains at the same time her bridge-playing friends and those who shun the game.

*   *   *   *

This life story has been interrupted to picture Wallis Simpson as she is known today in London. Her appearance, her tastes and opinions—these help to convey that picture. But those who would know Wallis Simpson as she is, should remember the heritage that is hers from ancestors who were courageous in battle, who lived in castles in ancient England and conferred with Kings, who came to a New World and, from that wilderness, wrested homes and wealth and important places in state and nation.

The picture is sketchy and incomplete. It is inserted because, only by keeping in mind the brilliant personality of Wallis Simpson, can events of recent years—events that have stirred the interest and quickened the hearts of men and women in Europe and America and far-flung outposts of civilization as nothing else in a decade or more—be understood.

Consider then, Wallis Simpson's story—

Chapter 10

❖

AN OCEAN liner, arriving in New York in the spring of
1933, had included on its passenger list the name of
"Mrs. Ernest Simpson of London."

The name was of no significance to ship news reporters and none of them asked for interviews. None of the
camera men who boarded the ship at Quarantine asked
Mrs. Simpson to pose for photographs, either. With little
ado, she passed through the customs offices, went to a
railroad terminal and took a train for Washington, D.C.

In Washington, Wallis Simpson went to the apartment
of her aunt, Mrs. D. Buchanan Merryman, who, since the
death of Wallis's mother, has been closer to her than any
other relative. It must have been an arrival that brought
quick memories, flashes of grief and happiness as Wallis
Simpson saw familiar streets and landmarks. Memories
of Washington in her little girlhood, her debutante days
. . . Washington before the war and afterward . . . the
days she lived in the little house in Georgetown . . . her
mother's funeral.

It was to visit her aunt that Wallis Simpson had come
to Washington. She saw, too, during her stay there her
cousins, Mrs. Anne Suydam and Mrs. Newbold Noyes,
and heard news of her uncle, Henry M. Warfield, living

in Baltimore. One afternoon Mrs. Simpson and Mrs. Merryman drove to Baltimore saw the races at Pimlico, and dined with friends.

There were parties in Washington for Mrs. Simpson. It was known that she had been presented at Court and had met the Prince of Wales. Old acquaintances and new ones asked eagerly for news of London, the fashionable life there and famous celebrities.

Wallis was delighted to be in her old home, friendly as she has always been, reticent about her success as a hostess abroad. She stayed on in Washington for a month, departed to spend a few days in New York before taking a boat again for England.

The night before she sailed there was a dinner in New York in her honor. One of the guests was George Marshall, owner of the new Roosevelt raceway at Westbury, L. I., who later married Corinne Griffith, the motion picture star.

Friends took Mrs. Simpson to her ship next day, and waved farewells. Sailing down New York harbor on that voyage, Wallis Simpson saw the Manhattan skyline for the last time. She has not returned to America since.

*   *   *   *

That fall when fashionable Londoners opened their town houses and newspaper social columns chronicled events of the new season and theaters were presenting new plays, Mr. and Mrs. Simpson were seen frequently with the Prince of Wales. Accompanying the Prince they attended the Embassy Club and Covent Garden. The Prince came to tea at the Simpsons' Bryanston Court apartment and Mr. and Mrs. Simpson received invitations to entertainments at St. James' Palace.

Those who know King Edward VIII and Mrs. Simpson explain that the friendship which developed between them is based on many mutual interests. The King who, all his life has been democratic, admires her naturalness and complete lack of pretense. Both like country life and the races and dancing. Both prefer informal to formal social functions. Mrs. Simpson's devotion to flowers and the King's fondness for gardening are allied. The King, then the Prince, found most appealing the atmosphere Mrs. Simpson creates in her home—an atmosphere of hospitality and comfort and simple friendliness.

In the summer of 1934 when the Prince of Wales set sail on the yacht, Rosaura, for a cruise of the Riviera, included among his guests was Wallis Simpson, chaperoned by her aunt, Mrs. Merryman.

From Cannes, Sept. 12, came this news report:

"The Prince of Wales is evidently enjoying his sojourn in Cannes, for today he decided to remain three days longer. He sent to Marseilles the airplane that had come to take him to Paris.

"To the delight of hundreds of onlookers, last night the Prince danced the rumba with an American woman, identified as a Mrs. Simpson.

"Although it had been announced that the Prince would stay aboard the yacht, Rosaura, he came ashore yesterday afternoon and, shortly before midnight, he appeared at the Palm Beach Casino with Mrs. Simpson and John Taylor, British Vice-consul at Cannes."

Three days later there was this report:

"Of all the invitations the Prince of Wales received during his stay at Cannes, he accepted only one. He was a guest for luncheon aboard the yacht of Mr. and Mrs. Sydney Allen of St. Louis who have been cruising these

waters recently. Other guests included Mr. and Mrs.
Herman Rogers, the latter the former Katharine Moore
of New York, and Major and Mrs. Douglas King. Mrs.
King, before her marriage, was Ruth Ady of Cincinnati."

The Mr. and Mrs. Herman Rogers referred to are the
friends who entertained Wallis Simpson in Peiping and
who, with her, were guests at Balmoral Castle in Sept.
1936.

In Feb., 1935, with other guests of the Prince of
Wales, Wallis Spencer attended the winter sports at
Kitzbuhl in Austria. News correspondents wrote from
Vienna:

"The Tyrolese winter sports resort at Kitzbuhl where
the Prince of Wales is expected Tuesday is already
crowded with Austrian aristocracy. Authorities are taking every precaution to be sure that the Prince's strict
incognito will be observed."

Another dispatch dated Budapest, stated:

"Budapest is suffering from Prince-of-Wales fever.
Since the British heir's arrival here last night the whole
population has been trying to get a glimpse of the royal
visitor."

*   *   *   *

In all that has been written about the friendship of
King Edward VIII and Wallis Simpson, much has been
said about Fort Belvidere, the King's country home.

Of all the castles and palaces where he has lived, Fort
Belvedere is said to be the King's favorite. It is but a
short motor trip from London—about 30 miles. Here,
weary of ceremony and state functions, Edward VIII can

live the life of a country gentleman. Here he likes to entertain his friends.

Judged by other royal residences, Fort Belvedere is small, though it covers a large acreage. It has a swimming pool and tennis courts. At the back of the Fort there are many lovely walks—grassy paths beneath vaulting trees. One of these natural lanes, winding on for some distance, comes at length to a picturesque old ruin in Grecian style.

It is at Fort Belvedere that King Edward indulges his fondness for gardening. The rhododendrons are his particular pride, enormous ones of handsome colors. The rooms at Fort Belvedere throughout the summer are always filled with flowers from the King's gardens.

Guests, coming for the week-end, usually arrive in the late afternoon at about the tea hour. They will be served tea in the drawing room, three sides of which are windows. It is a lovely room, creating the general impression of freshness and light. It is furnished with beautiful antique walnut, chintz in rich yellow shades, and on the walls there are a number of fine paintings by Italian and Dutch artists.

On one side of the room, before the windows, stands a long table, especially built to hold the King's jigsaw puzzles. Invariably these puzzles are the largest and most intricate to be obtained.

The dining room, which, like the living room, opens off a large central hallway, is a very masculine room. It has a long, beautifully carved walnut table that is never covered by linen or mats of any sort. There are ancestral paintings on the walls.

At dinner on Saturday nights at Fort Belvedere the King invariably wears Scotch attire. This consists of a kilt that may be one of many Scotch clans, worn with a tunic of dark cloth with beautiful silver buttons and a narrow inside collar of fine white lawn. It is, women friends declare, of all the monarch's innumerable uniforms and costumes, the most becoming.

An added Scotch touch to dinner at Fort Belvedere is the presence of the pipers who play while coffee is being served.

Like many bachelor hosts, King Edward, during a stay at Fort Belvedere, seats a different guest on his right each night. The entire visit is sure to be informal. Sunday luncheon is always a buffet meal, with servants appearing very little. On either side of the dining room there are two large buffets. Hot foods are placed on one and cold on the other. Guests make their own selections and serve themselves.

As in most other castles, each of the bedrooms is named—such names as "The Queen's Room," "The Blue Room" or "Prince William's Room."

*   *   *   *

Mr. and Mrs. Ernest Simpson were, in 1935, known as members of the Prince of Wales' intimate circle of friends. The list today is much the same as it was then, including: the Duke and Duchess of Sutherland; Lord and Lady Louis Mountbatten; Lord and Lady Brownlow; Lord Dudley; the Hon. A. Duff-Cooper and Lady Diana Duff-Cooper; the Hon. and Mrs. Evelyn Fitzgerald; Lady Cunard; and Mr. and Mrs. Colin Buist.

These are the names from which the guest list at Fort Belvedere usually is made. All are about the King's age, all have much the same tastes. Duff Cooper is the Minister of War in the British Cabinet and an author. Lady

Diana was the famous Lady Diana Manners of the stage. Lord Louis Mountbatten is, of course, a cousin of the King. The Sutherlands have both social eminence and wealth. Captain Fitzgerald, like Ernest Simpson, is a business man.

*   *   *   *

January 21, 1936 in London the cry rang out, "The King is dead; long live The King!"

Edward VIII, at the instant of the death of his father, George V, became his successor. A day later, with traditional pomp and ceremony, Edward VIII was proclaimed King. Londoners, bare-headed and tremulous with emotion, heard the fanfare of trumpets, the thunder of saluting guns, and then the reading of the official proclamation. Bands played the national anthem and voices rose in chorus:

"Send him victorious, happy and glorious
    Long to reign over us.
    God save the King—"

At once King Edward VIII took over duties of state. In March, in his first radio broadcast he paid an eloquent tribute to his father and then said:

"It now falls upon me to succeed him and carry on his work.

"I am better known to most of you as the Prince of Wales—as the man who, during the war and since, has had an opportunity of getting to know people in nearly every country of the world under all conditions and circumstances. And although I now speak to you as King, I am still that same man who has had that experience

and whose constant effort it will be to continue to pro-
mote the well-being of my fellowmen.

"May the future bring peace and understanding
throughout the world and prosperity and happiness to the
British Empire and may we be worthy of the heritage
that is ours."

It was a statement to give his subjects a glimpse of the
nature of their new monarch.

Another picture which should be recorded is that of
Westminster Abbey on Maundy Thursday, April 9.

Standing beside the Archbishop of Canterbury, Edward VIII that day distributed alms to 71 aged men and
71 women, some on crutches, many in worn and shabby
clothes.

It was the King's first public ceremony since his
father's funeral. The tradition, hundreds of years old, is
that on Maundy Thursday the king shall make gifts of
food, clothing and money to the poor and that there shall
be one man and one woman for every year of his age.

Edward VIII, however, had specified that 71 men and
71 women should be present to receive gifts—as many
as there would have been had King George been living.

Those who attended the ceremony say that, as the
King walked down the aisle, his eyes raised to the reserved section where Wallis Simpson was standing. His
gaze, clear and direct, did not leave her face until he
took his place beside the Archbishop and began distribut-
ing the bags of money.

*   *   *   *

The Court Circular, which gives to readers of English
newspapers a picture of events in the royal household

each day, contained a single paragraph Thursday, May 28, 1936.

Beneath the facsimile of the royal arms this paragraph read:

"The King gave a Dinner Party at St. James's Palace this evening to which the following had the honor of being invited: Commander the Lord Louis Mountbatten; the Right Hon. Stanley Baldwin, M.P., and Mrs. Baldwin; Colonel the Lord Wigram and Lady Wigram; the Right Hon. A. Duff Cooper, M.P., and the Lady Diana Cooper; Lieut. Colonel the Hon. Piers Legh and the Hon. Mrs. Legh; Lady Cunard; Admiral of the Fleet Sir Ernle Chatfield and Lady Chatfield; Colonel Charles Lindbergh and Mrs. Lindbergh; and Mr. and Mrs. Ernest Simpson."

It was news that caused much comment in London. There were further comments in August when King Edward set off with a group of friends for a cruise of the Adriatic on the "Nahlin," $1,350,000 yacht owned and leased to His Majesty by Lady Yule.

Lord and Lady Brownlow, Lady Diana Duff Cooper, and Mrs. Evelyn Fitzgerald were in the group. And so was Mrs. Simpson.

In the United States pictures of the King and his friends, photographed on the cruise, began to appear in newspapers. Almost invariably these photographs showed Wallis Simpson beside the King. There was never the slightest attempt on his part to prevent such pictures being made. On the contrary, stories are told of local police seizing press cameras, only to have the King himself hand the cameras back to their owners.

At the end of the cruise not a newspaper reader in the

United States was unaware of King Edward's friendship for Mrs. Simpson.

Back in England, the King spent some time at duties in London, then proceeded to Balmoral Castle in Scotland. The Court Circular a few days later announced that, at Balmoral, the King had guests—his brothers, the Duke of York and the Duke of Kent; the Duchess of York and the Duchess of Kent; the Duke and Duchess of Marlborough; the Duke and Duchess of Sutherland; the Duke and Duchess of Buccleuch and Queensberry; the Earl and Countess of Rosebery; Mr. and Mrs. Herman Rogers of New York; and Mrs. Simpson.

News wires added that when Mrs. Simpson and the Rogers arrived by train in Aberdeen the King was at the station to meet them, having driven 50 miles from Balmoral Castle, at the wheel of his own car.

When, a few days later, Mrs. Simpson returned to London she went to her new address on Cumberland Terrace. Ernest Simpson had moved, also, from the Bryanston Court apartment to the Guards' Club.

Still later—on October 14—wire services, familiar now with the name of Wallis Simpson, flashed that name around the world. It blazed in headlines, in two-inch type. Wallis Simpson, the headlines said, had filed suit for divorce.

Chapter 11

❖

DIVORCE

"I SWEAR by Almighty God the evidence I give to this court shall be the truth, the whole truth and nothing but the truth."

Hand uplifted, Wallis Simpson took the oath in the ancient Assize Court at Ipswich, England. She stood behind the oaken panels of the witness box, addressing stern, be-wigged Justice Sir John Anthony Hawke, in his robes of red, black and ermine. Beside him on the bench sat the high sheriff, face immobile. Above them was the wine-colored canopy.

Outside, police guarded the big double gate in the courtyard. Five more, headed by a sergeant, handled inspection passes at the outer door of the court room. And still seven more, four of them in plain clothes, faced the spectators near the press box, apparently on the outlook for cameras which had been barred. Smartly uniformed bailiffs were scattered throughout the courtroom.

It was the afternoon of Oct. 27, 1936. Guardsmen in scarlet tunics and black busbies had heralded the arrival of His Lordship Justice Hawke in court. The case of "Simpson W. vs Simpson E.A." was the first on the schedule for the day.

The town of Ipswich was thronged with visitors. Newspaper reporters and correspondents for foreign services and photographers and news reel camera men were there by scores—the photographers, many of them, perched on roofs, the news reel men forbidden to bring their cameras. Reporters, allowed inside the court room, were kept within a restricted area of seats.

Lean, bespectacled Norman Birkett, Mrs. Simpson's attorney, entered the court room with her, sat beside her at a corner of the big table until Mrs. Simpson was called to the witness stand. On his right was his assistant, Walter Frampton.

The drama began:

"My Lord," said Mr. Birkett, addressing Justice Hawke, "I appear in this case with my learned friend, Mr. Frampton. I call the petitioner at once."

Mrs. Simpson arose and walked to the witness box. A clerk on the Judge's dais stood also and a police constable handed to Mrs. Simpson a New Testament, told her to raise her right hand and repeat, after him, the oath.

The words came clearly, distinctly. Then, as Counselor Birkett spoke again, Mrs. Simpson faced him.

"Your names are Wallis Simpson? You are now living at Beech House, Felixstowe?"

"Yes."

"Is your town address 16 Cumberland Terrace in Regent's Park?"

"Yes."

"You were married to Ernest Aldrich Simpson July 21, 1928, at the Registry Office in the District of Chelsea?"

"Yes."

"And I think that afterwards you lived with him at 12 Upper Berkeley St. and Bryanston Court in London?"

"Yes."

"Has there been any issue of that marriage?"

"No."

"Did you live happily with the respondent until the autumn of 1934?"

"Yes."

"Was it at that time the respondent's manner changed toward you?"

"Yes."

"What was the change?"

"He was indifferent and often went away for week-ends alone."

"Did you complain about this?"

"Yes, I did."

"Did he continue to do what you complain of—going away alone and staying away week-ends?"

"Yes."

"On Christmas Day, 1934, did you find a note lying on your dressing table?"

"Yes."

The note was produced and passed up to the judge. Proceeding, Mrs. Simpson said that shortly after Easter of this year she received a letter in an envelope addressed to her although the contents appeared to be intended for her husband.

"Having read the contents of that letter," asked Mr. Birkett, "did you then consult your solicitor?"

"Yes."

"Upon your instructions, did they keep observations upon your husband?"

"Yes."

"Did they (the solicitors) report to you on the result of their observations?"

"Yes."

"Did you subsequently receive information upon which your petition in this present case is based?"

"Yes."

"On July 23 of this year did you write your husband this letter?" Mr. Birkett, as he spoke, picked up a letter and gave it to Mrs. Simpson. "Read the letter," he continued.

Mrs. Simpson read, rather slowly, "Dear Ernest; I have just learned that while you have been away, instead of being on business as you led me to believe, you have been staying at the Hotel Bray with a lady. I am sure you realize this is conduct which I cannot possibly overlook and must insist you do not continue to live here with me. This only confirms the suspicions I have had for a long time. I am therefore instructing my solicitors to take proceedings for divorce."

It was, Mrs. Simpson confirmed, the letter she had written to her husband.

Mr. Birkett then handed her a form, asking, "Would you just look at this registration form? In whose handwriting is the signature on that form?"

"Mr. Simpson's."

"Your husband's?"

"Yes."

"Is that in the name of Ernest Arthur Simmons?"

"Yes."

Mr. Birkett then turned, and, with a bow, said "Thank you". Mrs. Simpson returned to her seat and sat there, listening, as other witnesses were called.

The first was a waiter named Archibald Travers, employed at the Hotel de Paris in Bray. On July 21, 1936, he said, room number 4 of that hotel was in his charge

KING EDWARD VIII IN BRIGHT YELLOW SKIING ATTIRE, WITH MRS. SIMPSON AND
OTHER FRIENDS AT KITZBUHL, AUSTRIA, EARLY IN 1936

and was occupied by a man and woman to whom he served breakfast.

The waiter testified that the couple he saw in the room was the same couple he and another hotel employee, Dante Buscalia, saw on July 30, in the solicitors' offices in London. Counselor Frampton indicated Mrs. Simpson and asked if she was the woman. Travers said, "No."

A second waiter, Dante Buscalia, testified, that he, too had served the occupants of room number 4 in the Hotel de Paris, July 23. Counselor Frampton produced a photograph including Ernest Simpson and asked the witness if he recognized anyone in the picture.

Buscalia said that one of the persons was the man on which he had waited July 23.

The next witness, Christian Haesler, a hall porter at the hotel, testified that on the night of July 21 he received a man and woman and assigned them to room number 4.

"Did the gentleman sign the registration form?" the counselor asked.

"Yes."

"Did you produce it?"

"Yes."

"Did you see the gentleman sign the form?"

"Yes."

Norman Birkett then arose and addressed Justice Hawke, "Upon that evidence," he said, "I ask for a decree nisi with costs."

"Well," replied the judge, "I suppose that I must come to the conclusion that there was adultery in this case. There is one question which is in my mind. I think you know what it is."

"That the name of the lady has not been disclosed," said the counselor.

"That is it."

"But," went on Mr. Birkett, "the name is disclosed in the petition and she has been served with the petition."

"That was what was in my mind."

"If your Lordship pleases," Mr. Birkett then asked, "decree nisi with costs?"

"Very well. Decree nisi."

"Thank you, my Lord."

Mrs. Simpson, meanwhile, had left the courtroom and hurried to her automobile, waiting back of the Shire Hall. Newspaper reporters started to follow but all doors from the courtroom were locked. "Silence, silence!" shouted the bailiffs, and the reporters had to wait, because the doors were not opened until Mrs. Simpson's car had gone.

As the automobile emerged into Bond Street a police car blocked off other traffic. Police rushed toward two photographers and smashed their cameras. Mrs. Simpson's automobile continued to Felixstowe where she stopped for personal belongings and then, in a downpour of rain, set off again for Cumberland Terrace in London.

Servants there refused admittance to callers, and Mrs. Simpson remained in seclusion. She was not to be reached by telephone or message. She had nothing to say to reporters, and neither had Ernest Simpson.

But the report that the divorce had been granted spread by telegram and wireless and telephone. In the United States the news crowded the national presidential election and war in Europe from front page space. Pictures of Mrs. Simpson appeared and banner headlines. Yes, Mr. and Mrs. Ernest Simpson were divorced.

In city streets, in the rush of traffic, passers-by heard the name ring out. "Mrs. Simpson . . . Mrs. Simpson . . . Mrs. Simpson . . ."

And, as the word was spread and the news repeated and the headlines grew larger, there were newer reports. They began as whispers—at first discounted. They continued, they grew louder, they swelled.

"The King," said these reports, "is in love. The King and Mrs. Simpson will be married . . . He is going to make an American woman his Queen!"

Chapter 12

❖

FUTURE?

THE whole world asks the question, "Will King Edward VIII and Wallis Simpson be married?"

The world asks, too, if—in case of such a marriage—Wallis Simpson, American-born, will be Queen of England. When, if the marriage takes place, will it be solemnized? Who will perform the ceremony? Where will it be held and who will be present?

Or will Edward VIII, King of Great Britain and Emperor of India, renounce his throne for love?

It *is* love—deep and devout and sincere—between King Edward and Wallis Simpson. Of that the world is sure.

It is a romance to be compared with the great romances of the years. A devotion that is beautiful and overwhelming. Of a preciousness that rarely—so very rarely!—touches human lives, transforming them, by curious metamorphosis—and making of those lives a sort of poetry.

Yes, Edward VIII who, since boyhood has been the charmed darling of the world, "Britain's super-salesman," the "Bachelor Prince" who served in the war gallantly and rode recklessly and who danced and golfed and laughed with many girls but refused to enter a loveless marriage, for reasons of state, with any of them, has lost his heart—at last.

He has lost it to a commoner. American-born. A woman who has been married and divorced.

*   *   *   *

Wallis Simpson, secure and serene, at 16 Cumberland Terrace in Regent's Park, observes the conditions of her decree nisi divorce. Six months from Oct. 27, 1936, if the King's Proctor finds no cause otherwise, the nisi decree will be made final. Wallis Simpson, if she wishes, will be free to marry again.

And then—?

Authorities agree that there are no laws to prevent the British ruler from marrying whomever he chooses, so long as the bride is not of Roman Catholic faith. By the Bill of Rights, passed in 1689, a King of England who marries a Roman Catholic must surrender the throne to the next Protestant heir.

Wallis Simpson is not a Catholic.

She is a commoner, but this is no bar to marriage with royalty in England. Two of King Edward's brothers married commoners, and so did his sister, Princess Mary. The Duke of York, next in line of succession, married Lady Elizabeth Bowes-Lyon and the Duke of Gloucester married the daughter of the Duke of Buccleuch. Both brides were commoners. In England anyone has that rank who is neither royal nor a peer of the realm. Princess Mary's husband, the Earl of Harewood, was Lord Lascelles, a commoner, at the time of their marriage. Their two sons, also, are commoners.

There is the debated question whether or not a marriage between King Edward and Wallis Simpson could be sanctioned by the church.

The Church of England usually conducts royal weddings and it is usually the Archbishop of Canterbury who performs the ceremony. But the Archbishop of Canterbury has stated that it is his "desire that, in the case of any person previously married who has been separated by divorce from a husband or wife who is still alive, the marriage should not be solemnized in church."

More liberal churchmen believe, under certain circumstances, that such remarriages may take place.

*   *   *   *

No, there are no laws to make it impossible for King Edward and Wallis Simpson to wed. But there are barriers that can be stronger than laws. Barriers of tradition. Barriers of Empire. The slender threads, binding about the Crown, that hold together far-flung countries and varied races and nations. Political ambitions. Political factions.

Are these barriers so strong as to be insurmountable? Has the Old Order changed, so that no longer must Kings and Princes, by very virtue of their royal prerogatives, lose the rights of common men? Or has the changing world changed this, too? These are questions which wait for answers.

*   *   *   *

Kings have loved before—

Yes, Kings and Queens have loved and lost and won and suffered vain regrets and pulse-quickening exaltation, as other men and other women since the first year of the first ruler's reign.

Register and Tribune Syndicate

THE LIVING ROOM OF THE HOME IN WHICH MR. AND MRS. ERNEST
SIMPSON LIVED UNTIL A SHORT WHILE AGO

Pictures, Inc.

CUMBERLAND TERRACE, REGENT'S PARK, LONDON, THE PRESENT
HOME OF MRS. WALLIS SIMPSON

Kings have loved commoners and married them. Kings have loved those from whom, by creed and statute and station, they were separated—and some of them have married those loves, and some have not.

Kings have lost thrones for a woman's smile and, for love of country, they have renounced a lifetime's happiness.

Kings, in love, have become abject subjects, and those beloved have, by the same power, become rulers.

For romance knows no statutes, no peers, no parliaments, no press.

The world asks today, "Will King Edward marry Wallis Simpson? Will she, an American-born woman, be Queen of England?"

There is no answer until it comes from Buckingham Palace. Then America will know if Wallis Simpson is to be consort to the mightiest ruler on the earth and if she is to wear a crown. It would become her.

For Wallis Simpson IS a queen—the queen of romance, of glamor and the unfulfilled longings of a love-starved world. She is the queenly heroine of a love story that, touching these two—Edward VIII, monarch of the British Empire, and Wallis Simpson of America—touches millions.

A toast, America! A toast to THE QUEEN OF ROMANCE!